It's Beginning to Look a Lot Like COCKTAILS

Festive Favourites for the Most Wonderful Time of the Year

Jassy Davis

PAVILION

Pavilion
An imprint of HarperCollins*Publishers* Ltd
1 London Bridge Street
London SE1 9GF

www.harpercollins.co.uk

HarperCollins*Publishers*
Macken House
39/40 Mayor Street Upper,
Dublin 1
D01 C9W8
Ireland

10 9 8 7 6 5 4 3 2 1

First published in Great Britain by Pavilion
An imprint of HarperCollinsPublishers 2025

Copyright © Pavilion 2025
Written by Jassy Davis
Illustrated by Hannah Wood

Jassy Davis asserts the moral right to be
identified as the author of this work.
A catalogue record of this book is available
from the British Library.

ISBN 978-0-00-877009-9

Publishing Director: Laura Russell
Commissioning Editor: Caitlin Doyle
Editor: Shamar Gunning
Cover and interior designer: maru studio
Production Controller: Grace O'Byrne
Illustrator: Hannah Wood
Copyeditor: Helena Caldon
Reproduction: Rival Colour LTD

Printed and bound by PNB in Latvia

All rights reserved. No part of this publication
may be reproduced, stored in a retrieval
system, or transmitted, in any form or by any
means, electronic, mechanical, photocopying,
recording or otherwise, without the prior
written permission of the publishers.

Without limiting the author's and publisher's
exclusive rights, any unauthorised use of
this publication to train generative artificial
intelligence (AI) technologies is expressly
prohibited. HarperCollins also exercise their
rights under Article 4(3) of the Digital Single
Market Directive 2019/790 and expressly
reserve this publication from the text and data
mining exception.

This book contains FSC™ certified paper and other controlled
sources to ensure responsible forest management.

For more information visit: www.harpercollins.co.uk/green

DISCLAIMER
The publisher urges readers to drink responsibly.
This book features recipes that include the
optional use of raw eggs. Consuming raw eggs
may increase the risk of food-borne illness.
Individuals who are immunocompromised,
pregnant, or elderly should use caution.
Ensure eggs are fresh and meet local food-
standard requirements.

For Mum and Dad, who always made Christmas magical.

And to all fellow Christmas elves.

Welcome 5

Build Your Bar 6

Garnishes and Glassware 10

Ingredients Wish List 15

Syrups 17

The Recipes 22

- *Cocktails* 22
- *Pitcher Drinks* 102
- *Zero-proof Mocktails* 122

Index 142

Acknowledgements 144

This book is for everyone who brightens up when the nights start to grow long, because it means Christmas is on its way. The people who are ready with their festive decorations on 1 December. The ones who can't resist a 6-foot tree, even though their ceiling is only 5 foot 10 inches. The Christmas jumper-wearers. The carol-singers. The advent-calendar-makers. My kind of people.

I love Christmas. Unironically and unapologetically. I love the cinnamon- and pine-scented candles' smell of it. The boxes of iced cookies, the slabs of fruit cake, the tinsel and baubles, the heaped plates of roast meats, the 24/7 holiday movie channels, the gaudy window displays, the over-the-top light shows, and the piped Christmas tunes in every shop. Every single bit of the holiday season is beautiful to me.

The cocktails in this book are inspired by all of these wonderful festive things, as well as some of my favourite Christmas memories and Yuletide traditions from around the world. There are pitcher drinks for parties, alcohol-free options for the sober curious, and single-serve drinks for nights in reading Christmas romances or watching festive flicks.

You'll find cocktails based around everyone's favourite Christmas drinks, like Baileys and Advocaat, along with aromatic liquors with a midwinter vibe. Gingerbread features heavily. As does Champagne, cream, chocolate, and mulling spices (although not combined in one drink, thankfully). Indulgent and celebratory, these cocktails will fill you with a happy, festive glow.

So, if the approach of the end of the year fills you with joy, raise a glass. And wish season's greetings to each and every one.

Build Your Bar

Tools and Equipment

Not sure what equipment you need to start making cocktails? This guide to the more essential cocktail tools and implements will help you navigate the drinks section in your local homewares store.

Cocktail Shaker

A cocktail shaker quickly chills your drink while adding dilution. This is important when mixing drinks, as it mellows the alcohol and makes the finished drink smoother. It also affects the texture; a shaken cocktail should be light, airy, and frothy. There are three basic cocktail shakers to choose from: the Boston, the cobbler, and the French.

- **Boston shaker** – This is the classic two-piece shaker you'll typically see in bars. It consists of a large shaking tin and a smaller tin, also known as a pint glass. Boston shakers are big, so there's plenty of room for the drink and ice to move around inside it. The downside is that it can be tricky to seal and open, especially for novices. You'll also need to buy a separate strainer or two.

- **Cobbler shaker** – A three-piece shaker with everything you need included. There's a tin, a lid with an in-built strainer, and a cap to cover it. Perfect for beginners, and the shaker I still prefer to use when I'm mixing drinks at home.

- **French shaker** – This shaker has a tin and a lid but no in-built strainer, so you'll need to get a separate strainer to pour your drinks. It looks elegant and is a good stepping stone if you want to move on from a cobbler but don't want to tackle a Boston shaker just yet.

Mixing Glasses

When you want to stir rather than shake a cocktail, you need a mixing glass. Stirred drinks are normally all liquor without any mixers, like fruit juice or cream. Stirring is a way to chill and dilute your cocktail without adding aeration. A mixed drink should have a smooth, silky texture.

Choose a mixing glass that's wide enough to let you keep the bar spoon moving and deep enough to contain the cocktail without it spilling over the top.

A heavy base adds stability – you don't want the glass to topple over mid-stir. Etched mixing glasses can provide extra grip when you're holding them, and those with thick sides will insulate the drink from the warmth of your hands. A mixing glass with a spout is significantly easier to pour from than one without, so don't discount that when you're choosing your glass.

Bar Spoon

To go with your mixing glass, you'll need a bar spoon. These are long-stemmed spoons that typically have a 2.5–5ml / ½–1 teaspoon bowl and a long stem. There are three types of bar spoon: American, European, and Japanese.

- **American bar spoons** – The simplest kind of bar spoon, which has a rubber cap on the end and a twisted section in the middle of the stem. A good, basic option.

- **European bar spoons** – These spoons often have round, flat discs at the end, which can be used to muddle soft fruits. The stems are twisted all the way down. You can use them to layer drinks by trickling the spirit down the stem.

- **Japanese bar spoons** – These spoons have teardrop- or pearl-shaped tips and are much longer than their American and European counterparts, making them a lot more theatrical to use.

Jiggers and Measuring Glasses

A jigger is an hourglass-shaped measurer that has two measuring bowls – the standard jigger (45ml / 1½fl oz) and the pony (30ml / 1fl oz). These are the basic measurements for cocktail making. You can also buy small measuring glasses that are marked up with millimetres, fluid ounces, tablespoons, and teaspoons. They're great for precision measuring, and I always use one when I'm developing cocktail recipes.

Strainers

A strainer is often useful, even if you're using a cobbler shaker, and it's non-negotiable for Boston shakers, French shakers, and mixing glasses.

A Hawthorne strainer is a metal disc with a coiled spring attached to it. It catches large chunks of fruit or ice when the cocktail is poured out. It's perfect for straining cocktails from a shaking tin.

While a Hawthorne strainer works well with a mixing glass, the traditional strainer for them is a julep strainer. It has a handle and is shaped like a bowl or spoon but has holes stamped in it. The bowl shape cups the ice in the glass, holding it back more firmly than a Hawthorne strainer and making it easier to pour your drink. It's a neat way to take your bar cart to the next level, once you're comfortable with using it.

Sometimes a cocktail needs to be fine-strained. This means you'll need to pour your cocktail through both a Hawthorne or julep strainer and a fine-mesh sieve to catch very small pieces of fruit pulp, herbs, or chips of ice. Small, hand-held sieves, similar to tea strainers, are ideal for this.

Muddlers

Muddlers are used to crush soft fruits and herbs and to bruise citrus peel. They're usually made out of wood, plastic, or steel. Wood looks good and is tough. Plastic and steel have the benefit of being dishwasher-friendly.

Garnishing Tool

The secret to getting the perfect long strip of zest that you can twist and twirl is a canele cutter or channel knife. These are narrow peelers that smoothly pull long ribbons of peel off an orange or lemon, which you can then turn into the perfect twist. You can also use a regular vegetable peeler to peel strips off citrus fruits. See page 12 for advice on making twists.

Juicer

A big part of cocktail making is squeezing citrus fruits. A hand-held lemon juicer is a useful bit of kit to have in your cocktail cabinet.

Blenders

For frozen cocktails, a blender is essential. Choose a blender that's big enough and packs enough power – at least 1000 Watts. Blenders that promise they can crush ice and make smoothies are the best choice for cocktail making, as they're normally powerful and quick – the faster the blade spins, the finer your ingredients will be processed.

When it comes to making crushed ice, food processors usually do a better job than blenders. Although, the best crushed ice comes from the store.

Ice Cube Trays

You're going to need plenty of ice. You can buy it – normally the best option for parties – but making your own means you can vary the size and shape.

Oversized ice cubes are great for shorter, spirit-forward drinks like Old Fashioneds, while long, spear-shaped ice cubes can work in tall cocktails served in collins glasses. Really tiny ice cubes create a cobbled effect in the glass. If you're feeling festive, look out for ice cube trays that make ice in Christmas shapes, like trees, candy canes, and baubles. Cocktails should be fun, after all!

Glassware and Garnishes

Gorgeous Glasses

Using the right glass can make all the difference to your cocktail. A stemmed cocktail glass stops your hands warming the drink, while a coupe means you get a face full of aromatics when you lift the glass to your lips. If you're not sure which glass is what, follow this guide and then decide which kind you want to add to your bar cart first.

Highball and Collins Glasses

Highballs and collins glasses are both tall; the main difference is that highballs are thin, while collins glasses are wide. But the difference is small. Highballs usually hold 240–350ml / 8½–12fl oz of liquid, while collins glasses measure 350–450ml / 12–16fl oz. If you want to invest in just one tall glass, pick one that's 350ml / 12fl oz, that can also stand in for sling and hurricane glasses.

Rocks and Old Fashioned Glasses

Lowball tumblers come in two basic sizes: single rock and double rock – the latter of which is more commonly known as an old fashioned glass. Single rock glasses are 250–300ml / 8¾–10fl oz and will comfortably fit a chunk of ice and your drink. Old fashioned glasses are 300–350ml / 10½–12fl oz, and they make great midsize glasses for spirit-forward drinks served over ice, like Negronis (see page 32), or cocktails served with crushed ice. Old fashioned glasses can also stand in for julep tins.

Coupes, Nick & Nora, and Martini Glasses

For cocktails served 'up' (without ice), you need a stemmed glass to protect the chilled drink from the heat of your hands.

Coupes, or champagne saucers, are stemmed glasses with wide bowls. They normally hold around 180ml / 6fl oz and are a great choice for shaken cocktails. The wide surface area lets the cocktail breathe, so you can inhale the drink's scent as you sip.

Nick & Nora glasses are bell-shaped and elegant, with a touch of speakeasy glamour. They're smaller than coupes, at 120–140ml / 4–4¾fl oz, so they're great for small, strong cocktails that might vanish in a full-sized coupe.

V-shaped martini glasses come in a range of sizes, from elegant 120ml / 4fl oz to 180ml / 6fl oz and the bucket-like 250ml / 8¾fl oz. With cocktails, bigger is not necessarily better. The longer your cocktail sits in the glass, the warmer and less enjoyable to drink it becomes. This is especially true of spirit-forward drinks, like Martinis (see page 83) and Manhattans (see page 64). Err on the side of small to medium for the optimum Martini experience.

Copa, Wine, and Flute Glasses

Copa de Balon are gin and tonic glasses that evolved from red wine glasses in Spain. Their curved shape traps the gin's aroma while letting it breathe, and leaves space for interesting garnishes. They've become the go-to glass for Aperol Spritzes (see page 84), but a red wine glass with a wide bowl is just as good.

For Champagne cocktails, you should consider flute glasses. They hold around 180ml / 6fl oz, and the shape is meant to keep the bubbles fizzing. Coupes, by contrast, expose the surface of the drink to more air, which opens up the flavour but dampens the fizz. For the best flow of bubbles, go for a flute.

Hurricane, Sling, and Shot Glasses

The hurricane glass is a big glass, usually around 600ml / 21fl oz. It's named after hurricane lamps and is supposed to have been developed in New Orleans in the 1940s. It's the go-to glass for Tiki drinks and rum punches, like the Mele Kalikimaka (see page 44).

Elegant sling glasses look like highballs that have been squeezed and stretched. They're normally narrower at the base, with a flared rim, and measure 330ml / 11½fl oz. Sling glasses allow for plenty of ice, and they look stylish, especially if your cocktail is beautifully garnished.

A tray full of shot glasses can be useful for a party. A standard shot glass holds 300–450ml / 1–1½fl oz, while a double shot glass holds 60ml / 2fl oz. You can also use your shot glass as a measuring glass, so they work hard for their place on the bar cart.

Ornaments and Decorations

When it comes to making your cocktails look gorgeous, the final step is the garnish. At this time of year, every drink deserves to look its best.

Citrus Twists

Plenty of cocktails are simply garnished with a lemon, lime, or orange twist. There's a garnishing tool called a canele cutter/channel knife that makes preparing twists easy. Simply pull it along the skin of your citrus fruit, and it will create a long, thin ribbon of zest that's perfect for twisting.

There are two other ways to make a twist. The first is to cut a round slice from your citrus fruit, then cut a notch in it. Run your knife around the fruit pulp to cut it away from the peel. You should be able to open up the zest into a strip. Run the flat of your knife down the zest to slice away the white pith. Your twist is now ready to add to your drink.

Alternatively, use a vegetable peeler to peel a strip of zest off the fruit, then slice off any thick bits of pith. Use your knife to trim the edges to make it look neater. Strips of zest cut this way tend to be thicker and less flexible, so they're not as good for twists. They are, however, good for expressing and then dropping into a glass (see below).

To shape your ribbon of citrus zest into a twist, you can simply twist it or try wrapping the peel around a chopstick to create a spiral shape. Slide it off the chopstick, and the zest should hold its shape.

If you want to make lots of twists in advance for a party, shape them around a chopstick then drop them into a bowl of iced water. They should keep their shape and can be left in the water for a few hours, ready to use.

HOW TO EXPRESS A TWIST
When you express a twist, you're extracting the citrus oils from the zest. These will add aroma to your cocktail.

If your fruit has been coated in wax, make sure it has all been washed off. Better yet, choose fruit without wax. Then peel a strip of zest and slice away as much pith as possible. Use your thumbs and forefingers to hold the zest over your finished drink, skin-side down, then gently twist. An almost-invisible mist of citrus oil will spray over the surface.

Then rub the skin of your twist around the rim of your glass to coat it in the aromatic oil, and drop the twist into your glass.

Citrus Wheels, Slices, and Wedges

A slice of citrus is a very simple garnish that adds a pop of colour and an extra layer of aroma. A wheel is a round slice of citrus fruit, a slice is half a wheel, and a wedge is a thick chunk of citrus.

When you're cutting wheels and slices, use a small, sharp knife to cut them around ½cm (⅕in) thick. With wheels, you can cut an incision halfway into the round to make it easier to bend around the glass. For slices, just cut your wheel in half.

To make a wedge, cut your fruit in half then cut each half into quarters lengthways. Larger fruits, like grapefruits or big oranges, can be cut into six or eight wedges.

How to Salt/Sugar Rim a Glass

Coating the rim of a glass is very simple: just moisten the glass with a liquid, then dip and turn it in your chosen coating. Citrus juice is often used, but you can also use sugar syrup, egg whites, or flavoured spreads.

If you're using a lemon or lime wedge to wet your glass, cut a small slice in the flesh, then run that slice along the edge of your glass to coat it in juice. Otherwise, pour your liquid into a saucer and dip your glass into it.

Have your coating ingredient in a separate saucer. Dip the glass into it briefly to coat. You can also hold your glass at a 45-degree angle and turn it to coat the outside edges of the glass. This is a handy way to do it if you only want to coat half the glass.

Once your glass has its rim, put it to one side for a few minutes to let it set. If you can, leave the glass in the fridge; this will set the rim and also start to chill it, ready for your drink.

How to Smoke a Cocktail

There are three ways to add smoke to a cocktail. The first is to swap the Angostura bitters for a dash of smoke bitters. There are a few varieties available, and they're often a mix of oak and smoke. They have a peaty, woody flavour.

Alternatively, you can use a cocktail smoker. There are two types to choose from: a smoking gun or a smoke lid. I prefer a smoke lid, but a gun can be useful for doing several cocktails at once.

Smoke lids look like wooden flying saucers. They have a chamber in the middle, to which you add a pinch of wood chips. Place the lid on top of the glass, then light the wood chips with a cook's blow torch. Cover and let the smoke fill the glass for 30 seconds–1 minute, then remove the smoker and serve. Most smoke lids come with a mix of wood chips to use. I tried the Stuck up the Chimney on page 28 smoked with cherry wood and oak – both were great.

Whichever wood smoke you go for, just make sure you extinguish the wood chips properly before discarding them. You only want your cocktail billowing smoke, not your entire house.

Ingredients Wish List

Bar Cart Essentials

If you're writing your Christmas cocktail ingredients wish list but are not sure where to start, this guide will help you work out what to put into your shopping cart.

Picking Liquor

The first question most people ask when it comes to making cocktails is: how good does the liquor have to be? The short answer is that it really depends on how deep your pockets are.

You can make cocktails with the most expensive spirits or with bargain-basement booze from the bottom shelf. But the most expensive liquors don't always give the best results. Some top-end spirits – especially whiskies, rums, and brandies – are best enjoyed as they are or served simply over ice. Some premium gins or vodkas are at their best mixed only with tonic water or soda. They have too much flavour to blend well into mixed drinks.

On the other hand, cheap spirits can have too much heat because they're made with cheap grain alcohol. Any flavour they have is swallowed up by the burning sensation you get at the back of your throat. Fruit juices and syrups can do a lot to cover up cheap booze, but they can't work miracles.

Mass-produced, mid-tier spirits can be a good place to start if you're not sure what you like, or which spirit you're going to end up using more of. These can offer a basic standard against which you can judge other spirits.

The best option is to visit your local off licence, tell them what cocktail you're making, what your budget is, and ask for their advice. They can point you in the direction of spirits you won't find on the supermarket shelf, which will give your cocktails an extra lift.

Egg Whites or Aquafaba

Cocktails with a fluffy, white layer of foam have normally been shaken with either egg whites or aquafaba. These protein-rich liquids give your cocktails a richer texture, nicer mouthfeel, and a pretty layer of fluff on top.

Egg whites are the go-to liquid for this. You can use fresh egg whites or buy cartons of pasteurized egg whites. The cartons are an especially good idea if you're planning to shake a lot of cocktails at a party or if you want to make sure the egg whites are safer to consume. In general, raw egg whites are fine, but they do come with a small risk. People who are pregnant, elderly, or who have compromised immune systems are best drinking cocktails made with pasteurized eggs/egg whites or alternatives.

If you don't like the idea of adding raw egg whites to your drink, or you want a plant-based alternative, then aquafaba is what you need. It's the liquid you drain from a tin or jar of chickpeas. It has a slightly beany flavour, but once you shake it into a cocktail, it blends in beautifully and the foam is just as good as egg whites.

Bitters

Cocktail bitters are deeply concentrated infusions of herbs, roots, and spices that are used to add an extra layer of flavour to cocktails. Think of them as liquid spices. And because they're liquid, they blend into cocktails more easily than if you tried to shake something like dried cinnamon into your drink.

Bitters are made by infusing a neutral-tasting alcoholic spirit with something bitter – like gentian root or cinchona bark – and particular herbs, spices, or flavourings. Bitters come in a huge range of flavours now, from simple orange or chocolate to habanero chilli, smoke, and quince.

The most well-known bitters are Angostura bitters. Created in the nineteenth century as a cure for stomach complaints, they're a mix of gentian root and spices, including cardamom, cloves, and cinnamon. They give cocktails a spice-rack warmth and are also good simply shaken into a glass of chilled soda water. A bottle of Angostura bitters is always useful and seemingly lasts forever. (My bottle is entering its tenth year and is still going.)

Bitters are typically added to cocktails by the 'dash'. This just means a firm shake. To add them to a drink, hold the bottle over your cocktail tin and give the bitters a committed shake. Usually, you'll add 1–3 dashes per serving – depending on the drink.

Syrups

Stock up Your Syrups

Syrups are a bartender's secret weapon when it comes to mixing drinks. Used sparingly, a syrup can enhance a cocktail's flavour, smooth out the rough edges, or take the heat out of spirit-forward drinks.

The most useful syrup to have on hand is simple syrup. It's usually made with white sugar boiled with water to create a straightforward liquid sweetener. This syrup is an all-rounder that you can use in almost any cocktail when you want to balance out the flavours or add a dash more sweetness. Swap the white sugar for alternatives like Demerara or soft brown sugar to make syrups with richer, fudgier flavours.

Syrups can be more than just a sweetener. They're also a great way to add extra layers of flavour. Infusing syrups with herbs, spices, and fruit gives you an instant shot of aroma that will add extra oomph to your cocktails.

STERILIZING JARS AND BOTTLES

To sterilize glass jars and bottles, preheat your oven to 160°C/Fan 140°C/Gas Mark 3. Wash the jars and/or bottles in hot, soapy water (including the lids for the jars, if they have them), then rinse and place on a baking tray. Slide into the oven and heat for around 15 minutes. Take them out of the oven and let them cool until they're cold enough to handle, then add the syrup and seal before storing according to the recipe instructions.

SIMPLE SYRUP

MAKES APPROXIMATELY
450ML / 16FL OZ

250g / 8¾oz granulated sugar
250ml / 8¾fl oz water

1. Tip the sugar into a saucepan and pour in the water. Set the pan over a medium–high heat and bring the syrup to the boil, without stirring, then boil for 2 minutes.

2. After 2 minutes, take the pan off the heat and let the syrup cool in the pan. Transfer to a sterilized jar, bottle, or tub, then seal and store in the fridge for up to 1 month.

▲▲▲▲▲▲▲▲▲▲▲▲▲▲▲▲▲▲▲▲▲▲▲

MULLED SYRUP

MAKES APPROXIMATELY
450ML / 16FL OZ

250g / 8¾oz granulated sugar
250ml / 8¾fl oz water
1 orange
1 lemon
25g / 1oz piece of fresh ginger
8 whole cloves
2 cinnamon sticks

1. Tip the sugar into a saucepan and pour in the water. Quarter the orange and lemon and thickly slice the ginger, then add them all to the pan. Drop in the cloves and cinnamon sticks.

2. Set the pan over a medium–high heat and bring the syrup to the boil, without stirring. Once boiling, set your timer for 2 minutes. After 2 minutes, take the pan off the heat and let the syrup cool in the pan.

3. Strain the cooled syrup through a fine-mesh sieve into a jug and discard the spices, citrus fruit, and ginger. Transfer the syrup to a sterilized jar, bottle, or tub, then seal and store in the fridge for up to 1 month.

GINGERBREAD SYRUP

MAKES APPROXIMATELY
450ml / 16fl oz

250g / 8¾oz soft brown sugar
250ml / 8¾fl oz water
50g / 2oz piece of fresh ginger
1 cinnamon stick
10 whole cloves
¼ nutmeg

1. Tip the sugar into a saucepan and pour in the water. Thinly slice the ginger and add to the pan. Drop in the cinnamon and cloves. Grate in the nutmeg.

2. Set the pan over a medium–high heat and bring the syrup to the boil, without stirring. Boil for 2 minutes. After 2 minutes, take the pan off the heat and let the syrup cool in the pan.

3. Strain the cooled syrup through a fine-mesh sieve into a jug and discard the spices and ginger. Transfer to a sterilized jar, bottle, or tub, then seal and store in the fridge for up to 1 month.

CRANBERRY SYRUP

MAKES APPROXIMATELY
450ml / 16fl oz

250g / 8¾oz granulated sugar
250ml / 8¾fl oz water
200g / 7oz cranberries, fresh or frozen

1. Tip the sugar into a saucepan and pour in the water. Add the cranberries – defrosting frozen berries first. Set the pan over a low heat and gently warm the syrup so the pan is just steaming but isn't boiling. Gently cook the cranberries for 15–20 minutes until they're soft, but don't let them burst – this helps minimize the amount of pectin the cranberries release into the syrup. Too much pectin and you'll end up with cranberry jam rather than syrup.

2. After 15–20 minutes, take the pan off the heat and let the syrup cool. Strain the cooled syrup through a fine-mesh sieve into a jug and discard the cranberries. Pour the syrup into a sterilized jar, bottle, or tub, then seal and store in the fridge for up to 1 month.

Tip: The cranberries will still be edible after being cooked in the syrup, although they'll be less sweet than you'd expect. To avoid waste, use them to make cranberry sauce or add them to stuffing mixes.

PINEAPPLE SYRUP

MAKES APPROXIMATELY
200ML / 7FL OZ

250g / 8¾oz fresh pineapple
1 lemon
150g / 5oz granulated sugar

1. Slice the skin off the pineapple, then chop the flesh into small chunks. Scoop the pineapple pieces into a jar. Use a vegetable peeler to peel 2 large strips of zest off the lemon, leaving behind as much white pith as possible. Add these to the jar.

2. Tip the sugar into the jar, then seal it and shake to coat the pineapple in the sugar. Leave to sit at room temperature for 4–8 hours, giving the jar a shake every hour, until the sugar has dissolved. Now leave the jar to sit at room temperature for 24 hours to infuse the syrup.

3. After 24 hours, strain the syrup through a sieve into a bowl. Discard the pineapple and lemon zest. Pour the syrup into a sterilized jar, bottle, or tub, then seal and store in the fridge for up to 1 month.

Tip: You can eat the pineapple you used to flavour the syrup. It's sweet and tasty. Try it spooned over yogurt, pancakes, or ice cream.

BEER SYRUP

MAKES APPROXIMATELY
225ML / 8FL OZ

150g / 5oz soft brown sugar
300ml / 10½fl oz IPA beer

1. Tip the sugar into a saucepan and pour in the beer. Set the pan over a medium–low heat and bring to a gentle boil. Turn the heat down and gently simmer for 25–30 minutes, stirring occasionally, until the syrup has thickened a little. It should be syrupy and viscous but still free-flowing if you scoop a spoonful out of the pan.

2. Take the pan off the heat and let the syrup cool. Transfer to a sterilized jar, bottle, or tub, then seal and store in the fridge for up to 1 month.

Tip: I used IPA beer to make this syrup because this was the beer syrup I liked best. If you're not a fan of IPAs, you can make this syrup with your preferred style of beer – brown ales, pale ales, wheat beers, bitters, even sours. They'll all give you a slightly different result, but, as a rule, if you like the beer, then you'll like the syrup!

GUINNESS SYRUP

MAKES APPROXIMATELY 350ML (12FL OZ)

500ml / 17½fl oz Guinness or other stout
250g / 8¾oz granulated sugar
200g / 7oz Demerara sugar

1. Pour the Guinness into a saucepan and tip in the granulated and Demerara sugars. Place the saucepan over a medium heat and bring to a gentle boil. Turn the heat down and gently simmer for 25–30 minutes, stirring occasionally, until the syrup has thickened a little. It should be syrupy and viscous but still free-flowing if you scoop a spoonful out of the pan.

2. Take the pan off the heat and let the syrup cool. Transfer to a sterilized jar, bottle, or tub, then seal and store in the fridge for up to 1 month.

3. If you cook the Guinness Syrup for too long, it will end up turning into a thick Guinness caramel, which is delicious but difficult to mix into drinks. If that happens, don't despair; transfer the caramel to a tub and store it in the fridge. When you want to use it for a drink, scoop a spoonful out, pop it into a heatproof bowl, and add a dash of boiling water. Stir to melt the caramel, adding a drop more hot water if it's still too thick. It will thin out and you can then use it in your cocktails.

Festive recipes this way ☞

Snow Day

Serves 1

Nothing beats waking up to a blanket of freshly fallen snow. Everything's quiet. The light's soft and dreamy. And, if you're lucky, the roads are closed, the trains have stopped running, and there's no way you can go into work. This happened to me once, before working from home was a thing. London was so thickly coated in snow, there was nothing I could do but text my boss to let them know I couldn't come in, then call my friends to go sledging in the park. We gathered up every plastic bag and scrap of cardboard we could find, then went to the park and used these makeshift toboggans to slide down the hill, landing face-down in the snow. Then we had a snowball fight. We came home pink-cheeked and laughing, having stolen a day of fun from the middle of the week. I wanted to capture that feeling in a cocktail; this light, bright, vanilla-scented drink topped with a white drift of foam is cool and crisp, like the weather, and filled with fun.

- 45ml / 1½fl oz vanilla vodka
- 15ml / ½fl oz Galliano Autentico liqueur
- 30ml / 1fl oz fresh lemon juice
- 15ml / ½fl oz Simple Syrup (see page 18)
- 15ml / ½fl oz egg whites or aquafaba
- Lemon wheel, to garnish

1. Pour the vanilla vodka, Galliano, lemon juice, Simple Syrup, and egg whites or aquafaba into a cocktail shaker. Half-fill the tin with ice, seal, then shake for around 15 seconds or until the tin is frosty. Strain the cocktail into a clean, empty glass and discard the ice from the shaker.

2. Pour the cocktail mix back into the tin, seal, then shake again until the cocktail feels light and foamy.

3. Fill an old fashioned glass with ice and fine-strain in the cocktail. Tuck a lemon wheel into the glass so it peeks out over the top of the snowdrift of foam, then serve.

Gingerbread Old Fashioned

Serves 1

Gingerbread has long been a festive favourite. For hundreds of years, bakers across Europe have made gingerbread cakes and cookies whenever there was a festival or fair to celebrate. And while you can now find gingerbread in every country, Germany is renowned for it, especially at Christmas. There, St Nikolaus brings good children gingerbread treats and Christmas trees are decorated with gingerbread ornaments. Germany is also the originator of beautiful gingerbread houses. Bakers began making *lebkuchenhäuser* in the eighteenth century. After the Brothers Grimm published *Hansel & Gretel* in 1812, gingerbread houses became a Christmas staple. Something about a woman being driven to desperate measures by children destroying her home must have struck a chord with harassed *hausfraus* during the festive season. German immigrants took the tradition to America, and the custom has flourished ever since. If you don't want to spend hours making a gingerbread house, how about mixing a gingerbread-infused Old Fashioned instead? This is sweeter than a standard Old Fashioned because of the extra spoonful of Gingerbread Syrup (see page 19). The spicy notes of clove, cinnamon, and ginger mingle with the bourbon, while the Velvet Falernum adds a deep, musky warmth to the drink.

45ml / 1½fl oz bourbon
10ml / ½fl oz Velvet Falernum Liqueur
10ml / ½fl oz Gingerbread Syrup (see page 19)
3 dashes of toasted almond bitters
Crystallized ginger on a pick, to garnish

1. Place an old fashioned glass in the freezer to chill for 5–10 minutes.

2. Fill a mixing glass with ice. Pour in the bourbon, Velvet Falernum, and Gingerbread Syrup. Dash in the toasted almond bitters. Stir constantly for 45 seconds–1 minute, until the drink is well chilled.

3. Add a large ice cube to the chilled glass and strain in the cocktail. Garnish with crystallized ginger on a pick.

Rye Hard

Serves 1

When *Die Hard* was released in July 1988, there was no suggestion that it was a Christmas movie, even though it was set on Christmas Eve at one of the worst holiday parties ever held in LA. But in 2007, journalist Michael Agger contributed a short piece to a *Slate* article on unlikely Christmas movies. He argued that *Die Hard* is a Christmas movie, albeit one that's full of cynicism about the holiday season's material excesses. Since then an online debate has raged: is *Die Hard* a Christmas movie or is it just a movie set at Christmas? I think it is a Christmas movie because it's all about a bitter, lonely man learning that there's nothing more important than love, family, and community, while the money-hungry bad guys get punished. It's *A Christmas Carol*, but with more missiles and grenades. In tribute to NYPD beat cop John McClane, this riff on an Old Fashioned is sweetened with Guinness Syrup (see page 21) as a nod to his Irish heritage. It's also flavoured with chocolate and orange bitters to give the drink a dash of Christmas spice, making it peppery and chocolatey with a zingy touch of citrus. Perfect for sipping in front of your favourite Christmas flick.

60ml / 2fl oz rye whiskey
10ml / ½fl oz Guinness Syrup (see page 21)
2 dashes of chocolate bitters
1 dash of orange bitters
Orange twist, to garnish

1. Place an old fashioned glass in the freezer to chill for 5–10 minutes.

2. Fill a mixing glass with ice. Pour in the whiskey and Guinness Syrup. Dash in the chocolate and orange bitters. Stir constantly for 45 seconds–1 minute, until the drink is well chilled.

3. Take the old fashioned glass out of the freezer and add a large cube of ice. Strain in the cocktail. Take your orange twist and twist it over the drink to express some of the oils, then drop it into the glass and serve.

Stuck up the Chimney

Serves 1

When I was a child, there was only one way to get in touch with Santa, and that was by letter. On Christmas Eve, freshly scrubbed and wearing clean pyjamas, my sisters and I would write our letters to Father Christmas. Then we'd burn them on the fire in the living room. The embers would fly up the chimney all the way to the North Pole where, my dad promised, the elves could use magic to put them back together again so Santa would know what gifts we wanted. To thank Father Christmas, by the fireplace we'd leave a mince pie and a glass of cream sherry – two things my dad happens to love – with a carrot for Rudolph. The next day the treats we'd left would be gone, with gifts in their place. It goes to show how effective a chimney can be for communication, because that's a less-than-12-hour turnaround time from order to delivery. Even Amazon would struggle to beat that. Perhaps the reason I've always loved the cozy, comforting smell of a wood fire is down to those festive memories. This cocktail has a similar dash of ash and charcoal, due to it being smoked. I use a smoke lid to bring out the woodsy flavours of the bourbon. Smoke lids are a lot of fun to use; watching the smoke swirl and spill out of the glass feels magical. Like Christmas gifts that appear in the night.

60ml / 2fl oz bourbon
5ml / ¼fl oz maple syrup
3 dashes of Angostura bitters
Orange wheel, to garnish (optional)

*See page 14 for tips on smoking a cocktail.

1. Place an old fashioned glass in the freezer to chill for 5–10 minutes.

2. Fill a mixing glass with ice. Pour in the bourbon and maple syrup. Dash in the Angostura bitters. Stir constantly for 45 seconds–1 minute, until the drink is well chilled.

3. Take the old fashioned glass out of the freezer and strain in the cocktail. Use a cocktail smoker to smoke the drink* and serve straight away, with no ice. If you prefer it unsmoked, just add a large cube of ice and serve. Add an orange wheel as an optional garnish.

Marzipan Sour

Serves 1

The best bit of a Christmas cake is the layer of marzipan that sits between the dense fruit cake and the thick fondant icing. Every year my mum asks if we should have an uniced Christmas cake to go with the cheeseboard (a delicious combination) or an iced cake for a festive afternoon tea. I always choose the iced cake, just for the marzipan. But there's still never quite enough marzipan for me, so I also eat as much stollen as I can during Christmas. The thick slab of marzipan that sits swaddled by the sweet dough is this marzipan fanatic's idea of heaven. The East-German bakers, who've been making stollen at Christmas since the fifteenth century, used to have to pay the Pope a penance for using butter, milk, dried fruit, and nuts in their baking during Advent, when they should've been fasting. Worth every penny, I say. My love of marzipan has been translated into this riff on an Amaretto Sour, which loads in as much almond as possible. There's orgeat syrup and toasted almond bitters backing up the nutty flavour of the amaretto, plus a dash of brandy. Whenever I've made marzipan from scratch, brandy is the spirit that brings together the eggs, almonds, and sugar. This is a silky, nutty, golden-brown cocktail with a thick layer of foam on top. A slice of fruit cake on the side is optional.

- 45ml / 1½fl oz amaretto
- 30ml / 1fl oz fresh lemon juice
- 15ml / ½fl oz French brandy
- 15ml / ½fl oz egg whites or aquafaba
- 8ml / ¼fl oz orgeat
- 3 dashes of toasted almond bitters
- Lemon wheel and maraschino cherry on a pick, to garnish

1. Half-fill a cocktail shaker with ice, then pour in the amaretto, lemon juice, brandy, egg whites or aquafaba, and orgeat. Dash in the bitters. Seal and shake for around 15 seconds or until the tin is frosty. Strain the cocktail into a clean, empty glass and discard the ice from the cocktail shaker.

2. Pour the drink mix back into the tin, seal, then shake again until the cocktail feels light and foamy.

3. Fill an old fashioned glass with ice and strain in the cocktail. Garnish with a lemon wheel or slice and a maraschino cherry on a pick.

Buon Natale

Serves 1

These days, there's a Negroni to suit every taste, time of year, and occasion. So why not a Christmas one, too? Negronis have been knocking about since 1919, when Count Camillo Negroni dropped into his local bar and asked the bartender for an Americano with a bit more kick. The bartender, Fosco Scarselli, mixed gin and sweet vermouth, but instead of lengthening the drink with soda water, he added Campari. Not only was the drink now boozier, it was also a lot more bitter. This is why a Negroni can be a challenging cocktail for the novice drinker. Many a cocktail newbie has confidently walked into a bar, ordered a Negroni, taken a sip, then regretted all the life decisions that led to them making that choice. But once you get into the sweet-bitter, bracingly herbal flavour of this Italian classic, it will end up being your favourite cocktail. However, like eating olives or getting up at 5am to crush the day, Negronis take some getting used to. So, for Christmas, let's make the Negroni a bit more of a crowd-pleaser. Adding a generous slug of sloe gin to the mix tips the balance of flavours away from bitter and leads the drink more towards the sweeter end of the scale. It's still herbaceous and pungent, but the rough edges are rounded off.

30ml / 1fl oz sloe gin
20ml / ¾fl oz London Dry Gin
20ml / ¾fl oz sweet vermouth
20ml / ¾fl oz Campari
Orange wheel and rosemary sprig, to garnish

1. Fill an old fashioned glass with ice. Pour the sloe gin, London Dry Gin, sweet vermouth, and Campari into the glass. Use a bar spoon to stir for around 30 seconds to chill the drink.

2. Thread an orange wheel onto a sprig of rosemary, then drop that into the glass and serve.

Santa's Smash

Serves 1

Mint Julep's less-showy cousin, Smashes were popular in the USA from the 1830s until the 1850s. Anything could be smashed – brandy, whisky, gin – and the only real difference between a Smash and a Julep was the size. Smashes were smaller, and they also came with less garnish and fuss. They vanished off bar menus in the 1860s, until Dale DeGroff brought them back at New York's Rainbow Room in the 1990s. DeGroff made a key change to the original mix: he added fresh lemon juice. Now, if you see a Smash on a bar menu, you almost always find some citrus in the mix. This tangy Christmas riff on a Smash muddles mint with lemon juice and cranberries to create a zingy base for the brandy. When you're bruising the mint, don't be afraid to give it a few good whacks – the drink is called a Smash, after all. When the scent of the mint is drifting out of the cocktail shaker, it's ready for you to add the liquor. Bright pink and refreshing with a crisp finish, this holiday drink is especially good if you happen to be celebrating Christmas somewhere warm. And it's still good if you're not.

- 25ml / 1fl oz Simple Syrup (see page 18)
- 15ml / ½fl oz fresh lemon juice
- 5 fresh mint leaves
- 8 fresh whole cranberries
- 60ml / 2fl oz French brandy
- 2–5 fresh cranberries on a pick and mint sprigs, to garnish

1. Pour the Simple Syrup and lemon juice into a cocktail shaker. Add the mint leaves and cranberries. Muddle them to crush the cranberries and bruise the mint so it releases its aromas.

2. Add plenty of ice and pour in the brandy. Seal and shake well until the tin is frosty, around 30 seconds.

3. Fill a rocks glass with crushed ice and strain in the Smash. Thread a few fresh cranberries onto a pick and rest that on the glass. Tuck in a couple of mint sprigs and serve.

Christmas Past

Serves 1

Smooth, velvety, and a little bit cakey, this dessert cocktail was inspired by one of the oldest types of mixed drink: the Flip. Originating in seventeenth-century England, Flips were a mixture of fortified wine, sugar, and egg. They were beaten together and then heated with a hot poker, which the barman would plunge into the drink until it seethed and frothed. In a cold coaching inn, a steaming-hot Flip must've been a welcome dose of warmth for weary travellers arriving stiff and cold after a journey. Over time the poker was ditched and bartenders focused more on producing a silkily smooth drink. The key was pouring the drink back and forth between two glasses multiple times – flipping it – and making sure the egg was well beaten. A cocktail shaker and lots of elbow grease will take care of both those elements today. Flips don't usually contain cream, but it's Christmas and cream gives the cocktail a dash of Eggnog richness. This drink includes a whole raw egg, so please be mindful about safety for some drinkers, or look out for cartons of liquid pasteurized eggs to use in your drinks; 1 egg equates to around 45ml (1½fl oz) liquid egg.

- 30ml / 1fl oz light rum
- 30ml / 1fl oz ruby port
- 20ml / ¾fl oz Cranberry Syrup (see page 19)
- 15ml / ½fl oz double cream
- 1 small egg
- 2–5 whole cranberries on a pick, to garnish

1. Place a coupe glass in the freezer to chill for 5–10 minutes.

2. Half-fill a cocktail shaker with ice. Pour in the rum, port, Cranberry Syrup, and cream. Crack in the egg. Seal and shake for around 30 seconds or until the tin is frosty.

3. Strain the cocktail into a clean, empty glass and discard the ice from the cocktail shaker. Pour the drink mix back into the tin, seal, then shake again until the cocktail feels light and foamy.

4. Fine-strain the cocktail into the chilled coupe. Thread the cranberries onto a pick and rest on the rim. Serve straight away.

Blushing Elf

Serves 1

Watching her long-lost stepson pour maple syrup over his spaghetti in *Elf*, Emily Hobbs asks him curiously: 'You like sugar, huh?' Buddy the Elf doesn't just like sugar, he LOVES it. Like all elfkind. According to Buddy, there are four main food groups that elves try to eat daily: candy, candy cane, candy corns, and syrup. This means that a cocktail for elves has to sit at the sugary end of the cocktail menu if Santa's sweet-toothed little helpers are to be persuaded to try it. Naturally, when coming up with an elf-themed cocktail, I started with maple syrup. I added some maraschino, a sweet cherry liqueur that mixes with the fresh lemon juice to give the drink the rose-like flavour of Turkish delight. The bourbon brings notes of oak and vanilla, as well as a dash of boozy heat. Crowned with a layer of fluffy, white foam, it's a deliciously syrupy cocktail that seems harmless while still putting plenty of colour in your cheeks. Drink it wisely – don't make the same mistake Buddy made when trying booze for the first time: tickle-fighting a prisoner on day release, Cossack dancing on a table in the mailroom, then arguing with his dad and running away from home. Unless that's the kind of Christmas you're aiming for. In which case, help yourself to seconds.

- 45ml / 1½fl oz bourbon
- 25ml / 1fl oz maraschino liqueur
- 20ml / ¾fl oz fresh lemon juice
- 15ml / ½fl oz egg whites or aquafaba
- 10ml / ½fl oz maple syrup
- Maraschino cherry, to garnish

1. Half-fill a cocktail shaker with ice. Pour in the bourbon, maraschino liqueur, lemon juice, egg whites or aquafaba, and maple syrup. Seal and shake for 30 seconds or until the tin is frosty.

2. Strain the cocktail into a clean, empty glass and discard the ice from the cocktail shaker.

3. Pour the cocktail mix back into the empty tin, seal, then shake again until the cocktail feels light and foamy.

4. Fill a rocks glass with ice cubes and strain in the cocktail. Drop in a maraschino cherry and serve.

Snow Globe

Serves 2

Cocktails are about theatre as much as they're about booze, and these glittering drinks have plenty of razzle-dazzle. They take a bit of prep, but you can set up your glasses the night before and just have them in the freezer, ready to go. This recipe serves two, but you could easily double it to serve four or more. It's also a fairly low-ABV drink, which can be useful for parties – the choice doesn't always have to be between alcohol and no alcohol. A long drink like this, with just a touch of liquor, is a great compromise. If you prefer your drinks strong, double the eau de vie, lemon juice, and Simple Syrup and halve the soda water. When it comes to eau de vie, use the best you can buy. The crisp, juicy sweetness of the pears in the Poire William eau de vie is what gives this drink its flavour.

2 sprigs of rosemary
20–30 fresh cranberries
60ml / 2fl oz Poire William eau de vie
30ml / 1fl oz fresh lemon juice
15ml / ½fl oz Simple Syrup (see page 18)
200ml / 7fl oz soda water, chilled
Edible glitter flakes, to garnish

1. Pour enough water into two balloon glasses to create a ½cm / 0.2in layer in the glass base. Trim the rosemary sprigs so you have 3–5 sets of leaves. Divide the cranberries among the glasses, then push a sprig into each glass, using the cranberries to hold them in place. The sprigs need to be 'upside down', with the snipped end at the top so the leaves flow downwards, looking like mini pine trees. Freeze the glasses for at least 2–3 hours or until the water in the glass is frozen and the rosemary is set in place.

2. When you're ready to serve, fill a cocktail shaker with ice. Pour in the eau de vie, lemon juice, and Simple Syrup. Seal, then shake until the tin is frosty, around 30 seconds.

3. Strain the cocktail into the glasses, then top up with soda water. Don't fill right to the top; you don't want the drink to spill when swirled.

4. Drop a pinch of glitter into each glass. Gently stir to create flurries. Serve straight away.

Make It for a Crowd

For a holiday get-together, multiply the quantities by the number of desired servings, then combine the vodka, lime juice, and cranberry juice into a 'mix' in a large pitcher. Chill in the fridge for 4–6 hours. To serve, fill each glass with crushed ice, add the mix, then top up with ginger beer. Try making bottles of the mix, which can be sealed and kept in the fridge for a couple of days, ready to pour.

Cranberry Christmas Mule

Serves 1

This might just be the perfect Christmas party drink. Crisp, fruity, dry, and a little fiery, it's easy to sip and simple to mix. It's a festive twist on a Moscow Mule, the classic party drink that was invented in 1941 by Wes Price, head bartender at the Cock 'n Bull Pub in Los Angeles. Price had been clearing out the bar's basement and needed a way to use up several crates of ginger beer that he'd found cluttering up the place. His solution: a long drink that mixed vodka, lime, and ginger beer. It was an immediate hit with the movers and shakers on the Sunset Strip. By 1942, Hollywood gossip magazines were hailing Moscow Mules as the hottest drink on the party scene. And when Hollywood loves something, it's guaranteed to take off with the rest of the world. Although the Moscow Mule does go in and out of fashion, it never fully disappears off bar menus; it's just too much fun. This Christmas version adds a slug of cranberry juice, which makes it extra tangy as well as cheerfully pink. Frothy and refreshing, it's a great drink for holiday get-togethers and also makes a delicious single-serve when you're having a party for one.

- 45ml / 1½fl oz vodka
- 15ml / ½fl oz fresh lime juice
- 50ml / 1¾fl oz cranberry juice drink, chilled
- 50ml / 1¾fl oz ginger beer, chilled
- Lime slice and fresh cranberries, to garnish

1. Fill a mule mug or collins glass with crushed ice. Pour in the vodka, lime juice, and cranberry juice. Use a bar spoon to stir everything together for around 30 seconds. The ice will start to melt as you stir, diluting the drink a little.

2. Add some more crushed ice to the glass, then top up the drink with chilled ginger beer. Give the drink an extra gentle stir. Either drop the lime and cranberries into the glass or thread onto a pick resting on the rim and serve.

Mele Kalikimaka

Serves 1

In 1949, a stenographer working in the office of Hawaiian businessman Robert Alexander Anderson wistfully complained about the lack of Hawaiian Christmas songs. There were hymns they could all sing along to, but no original island tunes. This caught Anderson's attention. He may have had a day job in an office, but he was also a brilliant composer who'd been writing hit songs since his student days. He got straight to work. The result was *Mele Kalikimaka*, a Hawaiian festive melody that gets its title from a literal, letter-by-letter translation of 'Merry Christmas' into Hawaiian. Anderson showed the song to his golf partner, who happened to be Bing Crosby. He loved it. The next year Crosby surprised Anderson by recording the song with The Andrews Sisters. And in 1955 he added it to a reissue of his compilation album *Merry Christmas*, supplementing the traditional mix of snow and sleighbell tunes with some much-needed sunshine. To match *Mele Kalikimaka*'s upbeat, beachy vibes, I've come up with a Tiki-style cocktail that's lusciously tangy. The combination of light and dark rums gives it a warm heart, while the Cointreau and passionfruit liqueur pile in the fruit notes. Even if you're not celebrating your Christmas on a golden beach under swaying palm fronds, this drink will make you feel like you are.

45ml / 1½fl oz light rum
15ml / ½fl oz dark rum
25ml / 1fl oz Cointreau
25ml / 1fl oz passionfruit liqueur
15ml / ½fl oz fresh lime juice
15ml / ½fl oz orgeat
Passionfruit half and mint sprig, to garnish

1. Pour the light and dark rums, the Cointreau, passionfruit liqueur, lime juice, and orgeat into a cocktail shaker. Half-fill the tin with ice, seal, then shake for around 15 seconds or until the tin is frosty.

2. Fill a hurricane glass with crushed ice. Strain in the cocktail. Rest a passionfruit half on top of the ice and tuck in a mint sprig. Serve with (optional) reusable straws.

Rudolph's Rum Swizzle

Serves 1

After a long night flying around the world delivering presents, a reindeer deserves to put up his hooves and enjoy a delicious mixed drink. Grassy and herbal, this refreshing cocktail balances the sweetness of port with a funky dash of hay, thanks to the combination of Angostura bitters and Velvet Falernum. They seem like flavours that would appeal to a magical reindeer, and maybe a few humans, too. A liqueur from Barbados, Velvet Falernum is typically infused with cloves, almonds, and lime zest. Sweet, mellow, and spicy, it's a key ingredient in West Indian rum cocktails, like the Swizzle. At its most basic, a Rum Swizzle is a simple mix of rum, water, and sugar mixed together with a swizzle stick. Originally, this would have been a short branch snapped off the *Quararibea turbinata* tree. The branches have stubby prongs that are perfect for mixing drinks, as well as an aromatic bark that adds a spicy bitterness. These days, wooden swizzle sticks have bark removed or they're made of plastic or silver. So instead, you'll find bitters on a Swizzle's ingredient list. Be reassured – you don't have to buy a swizzle stick to make this cocktail. A bar spoon will work just as well.

- 45ml / 1½fl oz golden rum
- 25ml / 1fl oz Velvet Falernum Liqueur
- 15ml / ½fl oz ruby port
- 15ml / ½fl oz fresh lime juice
- 8ml / ¼fl oz Simple Syrup (see page 18)
- 3 dashes of Angostura bitters
- Lime wedge and fresh cranberries on a pick, to garnish

1. Half-fill a sling glass with crushed ice. Pour in the rum, Velvet Falernum, port, lime juice, and Simple Syrup. Dash in the Angostura bitters.

2. Push a swizzle stick or bar spoon into the middle of the glass, then hold the stem between the palms of your hands. Rotate it quickly by sliding your hands back and forth for 30–45 seconds, or until the glass is frosty and well chilled. Top up the glass with more crushed ice, then swizzle again for 15–20 seconds.

3. Thread a lime wedge and fresh cranberries onto a cocktail pick. Rest it on the glass and serve with (optional) reusable straws.

Olive Oil Martini

Serves 2

In the depths of winter, there are many festivals of light. One is Hanukkah, the Jewish holiday commemorating the miracle of the oil in the second century BC. When Judah Maccabeus, leader of the revolt against the Greeks, entered the Second Temple of Jerusalem to restore it, he realized there was only enough consecrated oil left to burn for one night. He lit it anyway. Miraculously, the jar burned for eight days, in which time more consecrated oil was found. Consequently, oil and oily treats feature heavily in Hannukah traditions. I've been fortunate to join friends' celebrations, which always involve plenty of donuts and latkes. Two of these friends – Jo and Jordi – like a Martini. I came up with this olive-oil-washed riff on a Vesper Martini in their honour. 'Washing' the alcohol overnight with olive oil softens the liquor and takes out some of the heat. It also adds flavour, which varies depending on the olive oil you use. Use good-quality gin and vodka in this; I prefer a lighter, more herbaceous oil, which gives the drink a fresh, green aroma.

- 60ml / 2fl oz good-quality London Dry Gin
- 60ml / 2fl oz good-quality vodka
- 15ml / ½fl oz extra virgin olive oil
- 20ml / ¾fl oz dry vermouth
- 4 dashes of olive bitters
- Green olives on picks, to garnish

1. To make the olive-oil-washed spirits, pour the gin and vodka into a clean jar. Add the olive oil. Seal the jar, then shake well to combine. Leave on the worktop for 4–8 hours, giving it a shake whenever you pass. Place in your freezer for 12–24 hours.

2. When you're ready to serve, place two martini glasses in the freezer to chill. Take the olive-oil-washed liquor out of the freezer and remove the plug of frozen olive oil.

3. Half-fill a mixing glass with ice and pour in the vermouth. Stir a few times with a bar spoon to coat. Pour in the liquor, then dash in the olive bitters. Stir for 30 seconds.

4. Fine-strain the drink into the chilled glasses. Thread olives onto picks, drop into the glasses, and serve.

Sugar Cookie Cocktail

Serves 1

Crisp, buttery, sugar cookies are another Christmas tradition we can thank the Germans for. *Weihnachtsbäckerei* – Christmas baking – has been a much-loved custom in the German region for centuries; and when German immigrants arrived in America in the 1700s, they brought their cookie moulds and cutters. By 1796, the festive treat was well-enough known to appear in the first American cookbook, *American Cookery* by Amelia Simmons. Simmons warns that the cookies will be hard and dry straight out of the oven, so they're best left in an earthenware pot for a few months to soften. Sugar cookie technology has progressed since then, and baking them is now a key part of the holiday season for many. Inspired by that tradition, this creamy dessert cocktail tastes like caramelized sugar and spice and smells like walking into a bakery on a chilly winter morning. The combination of nutty amaretto and vanilla-scented RumChata backs up the buttery richness of the Biscoff Spread, which is made from crushed biscuits. The sprinkles garnish is a little bit extra, but if ever there's a time to go all out, it's Christmas.

2 tbsp Biscoff Smooth Spread
Multicoloured sprinkles, to garnish
25ml / 1fl oz amaretto
25ml / 1fl oz RumChata Cream Liqueur
25ml / 1fl oz single cream

1. Spread 1 tablespoon of Biscoff Smooth Spread around the rim of a martini glass. Tip the sprinkles into a saucer, then turn the glass upside down into them to coat the Biscoff-coated rim. Leave the glass to chill for 30 minutes to set the rim in place.

2. To make the drink, add the remaining 1 tablespoon of Biscoff Smooth Spread to a cocktail shaker. Pour in the amaretto and stir together until the Biscoff has loosened. Pour in the RumChata and single cream. Half-fill the tin with ice, seal, then shake for around 15 seconds or until the tin is frosty.

3. Fine-strain the cocktail into the decorated martini glass and serve.

Candy Cane Martini

Serves 1

Hot pink and fruity, this riff on a Cosmopolitan is the drink every holiday party needs. Instead of vodka – the main liquor in a classic Cosmo – this cocktail is made with peppermint schnapps. You may not expect peppermint to go with cranberry, but be prepared to be wrong. The sweet-shop stickiness of the schnapps and the mouth-drying tanginess of cranberry sit at such opposite ends of the flavour spectrum, they balance each other out brilliantly. It's an enemies-to-lovers kind of a vibe. And what is Christmas if not to bring adversaries together and then find a way for them to work things out? Even though this cocktail is great for a crowd, this is a single-serve recipe because I think it's perfect for that all-important festive tradition: the Christmas bubble bath. Just add a glass of water on the side (hydration is key), put on some Michael Bublé tunes, and settle in to enjoy an indulgently festive soak. If, after your bath, you decide this is a drink to share with friends, follow the instructions below to turn it into a pitcher drink.

Crushed candy cane, to garnish
8ml / ¼fl oz Cranberry Syrup, plus 2 tsp (see page 19)
60ml / 2fl oz peppermint schnapps
30ml / 1fl oz cranberry juice
15ml / ½fl oz fresh lime juice
3 dashes of orange bitters

1. Break a candy cane into small chunks, then crush into crumbs in a food processor or pestle and mortar or pop it in a bag and bash with a hammer or rolling pin. Tip the crumbs onto a plate.

2. Pour 2 teaspoons of Cranberry Syrup onto a saucer. Dip the rim of a coupe or martini glass into the syrup, turning to coat it, then dip it into the crushed candy cane. Leave the glass in the fridge to chill for 30 minutes for the rim to set.

3. Pour the peppermint schnapps, cranberry juice, lime juice, and the 8ml / ¼fl oz of Cranberry Syrup into a cocktail shaker. Half-fill it with ice and dash in the orange bitters, then seal and shake for around 15 seconds or until the tin is frosty.

4. Double-strain into the decorated glass and serve.

Make It for a Crowd

To mix for a crowd, multiply the ingredients by the number of guests, then stir everything over ice in a mixing glass (you may need to do this in batches) until well chilled. Strain into a pitcher, then store in the fridge for 2–4 hours. Decorate your glasses with the candy cane powder and keep them in the fridge. When the guests arrive, simply pour, and get the party started.

Rudolph's Rocket Fuel

Serves 1

There are different kinds of Christmases. There are picture-perfect holidays with angelic children opening gifts around a Christmas tree, straight out of a Hollywood movie. There are solemn religious services lit by candlelight with carols sung sweetly into the midnight air. And there are riotous 'Misrule' celebrations that, with a nod to this ancient tradition, are full of raucous fun and wild revelry. This cocktail taps into the spirit of the latter. My favourite Misrule story comes from 1329, when the clergy and choirboys at Exeter Cathedral in England behaved so badly during the Feast of the Holy Innocents (28 December) that the congregation fell 'into disorderly laughter and illicit mirth'. The church service ended in literal mudslinging, and the Bishop was forced to scold everyone for their high jinks. If that's the sort of atmosphere you'd like to bring to your Christmas events, this lively cocktail is for you. A punchy mix of bitter herbs, syrupy sweetness, and fizz with a twist of liquorice from the absinthe, it tastes exactly like something a student would drink before hitting the bars and clubs in search of a Christmas kiss. It's disco fuel and it's not for the weak.

45ml / 1½fl oz vodka
25ml / 1fl oz apricot brandy
15ml / ½fl oz sweet red vermouth
1 tsp absinthe
75ml / 2½fl oz Red Bull, chilled
Lemon twist, to garnish

1. Place a rocks glass in the freezer to chill for 5–10 minutes.

2. Pour the vodka, apricot brandy, and red vermouth into a mixing glass. Add ice and stir for 30–45 seconds to chill.

3. Take the glass out of the freezer. Add the absinthe and turn the glass to coat the inside with it. Tip out any excess absinthe.

4. Add a handful of ice to the glass. Strain in the cocktail, then top up with chilled Red Bull. Drop a lemon twist into the glass and serve.

Clementine Margarita

Serves 1

Sugar mice, chocolate coins, and a clementine – if that's what you woke up to in your stocking on Christmas morning, then you have been very good this year. In the UK clementine season begins in mid-October and ends around February. By December, they're at their peak. Clems have a sweet, delicate, citrus flavour with a hint of perfume. They're one of the key flavours of Christmas for me and I wanted to put them in a Margarita, but I found that the cleanness of silver tequila didn't bring out enough of the fruit's aromatic juiciness. Enter reposado tequila. Aged from two months to one year in barrels – usually either steel or American oak – reposado tequila has a warmth and richness that marries deliciously with the zestiness of clementine juice. Especially with a splash of Velvet Falernum in the mix. Try to buy reposado tequila that has been rested in oak, as the caramel and vanilla flavours from the wood will help give this festive twist on a Marg extra depth and richness. I didn't include a sweetener because I like the drink's crisp freshness. You can add 5ml / ¼fl oz Simple Syrup if you'd rather have it a touch sweeter.

45ml / 1½fl oz reposado tequila
25ml / 1fl oz Velvet Falernum Liqueur
15ml / ½fl oz clementine juice
8ml / ¼fl oz fresh lime juice
5ml / ¼fl oz Simple Syrup (optional) (see page 18)
Clementine wheel, to garnish

1. Place a coupe glass in the freezer to chill for 5–10 minutes.

2. Pour the tequila, Velvet Falernum, clementine and lime juices, and Simple Syrup (if using) into a cocktail shaker. Half-fill the tin with ice, seal, then shake for around 15 seconds or until the tin is frosty.

3. Double-strain the Margarita into the chilled glass. Add a clementine wheel to the drink and serve.

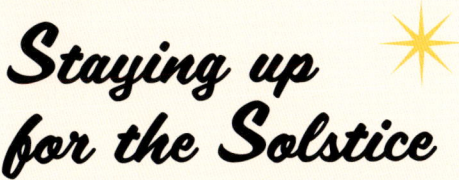

Serves 1

Staying up for the Solstice

In the Northern Hemisphere the longest night of the year is normally 21 December. You'd think that the day on which the sunlight trickles away and the dark takes over would be a time everyone would hide from, but the Winter Solstice is often a great night for a party. Traditionally, this is because we want to coax the sun to come back, so we put on a tempting spread of ritual dances, recitals, and ceremonies while lighting lots of candles and fires. The more lights we shine, the more likely the sun is to return. Or so the theory goes. But it's also because winter can be miserable, and nothing cheers everyone up like a shindig. If you're flagging – and who isn't in December? – then a midnight-black Espresso Martini topped with a creamy café au lait foam will perk you back up. This version is sweetened with a caramelly Guinness Syrup (see page 21) and Tuaca, a Renaissance Italian liqueur flavoured with oranges and vanilla. It's a sleek mix of bitter coffee and winter spice.

50ml / 1¾fl oz vanilla vodka
25ml / 1fl oz Tuaca Liqueur
25ml / 1fl oz hot, freshly brewed espresso
15ml / ½fl oz Guinness Syrup (see page 21)
3 coffee beans, to garnish

1. Put a coupe or martini glass into the freezer to chill for 5–10 minutes.

2. Half-fill a cocktail shaker with ice and pour in the vodka, Tuaca, espresso, and Guinness Syrup. Seal, then shake together vigorously for 30 seconds or until the tin is frosty.

3. Strain the cocktail into the chilled glass. Top with 3 coffee beans and serve.

Snow in the City

Serves 1

When snow falls in London, the city stops. I once spent 2½ hours walking home late one night due to an unexpected blizzard. It had been a typical cold, dark, midwinter evening when we'd gone into a club. By midnight, the street was blanketed in snow, and it was very, very quiet. No trains. No buses. No taxis. Just the sound of Londoners alternating between whoops of joy while throwing snowballs and complaining that 'Nothing works in this city and what are we meant to do now?' Luckily, I'm a flat-footwear-to-clubs kind of a gal, so I could trudge home through the snow with my friends. It was magical. Everything glittered. No sounds apart from the crunch of new snow. Occasionally, we'd meet a knot of students who'd been woken up by the eerie silence and run outside to make snowmen at 2am. Back home, we brought the feeling back into our fingertips with mugs of tea and hot-water bottles. When I woke up the next morning, the pristine white snow was already streaked with mud. Churned into slush by pedestrians and cars determined to inch their way through what had, briefly, been a winter wonderland. Snow in the city isn't pretty for long. This muddy-looking Espresso Martini embodies that messy, London-in-the-snow vibe. It's smooth and aromatic with a dash of winter magic.

50ml / 1¾fl oz vanilla vodka
25ml / 1fl oz coffee liqueur
25ml / 1fl oz hot, freshly brewed espresso
25ml / 1fl oz RumChata Cream Liqueur
Cocoa powder, to garnish

1. Put a coupe glass in the freezer to chill for 5–10 minutes.

2. Half-fill a cocktail shaker with ice and pour in the vanilla vodka, coffee liqueur, espresso, and RumChata. Seal, then shake together for 30 seconds or until the tin is frosty.

3. Strain the cocktail into the chilled glass. Dust with cocoa powder to garnish and serve.

Polar Espresso Martini

Serves 1

Has any drink conquered Christmas more thoroughly than Baileys? It's the world's best-selling liqueur, and almost half of those sales happen in the six weeks before Christmas. It wasn't originally intended to be a Christmas drink – even though it was launched in November 1974, just in time for the party season. Baileys was invented because the Irish government was offering generous tax breaks on successful export products. Gilbeys of Ireland had spirits to shift, so they asked a team of developers to come up with a new export drink. Two consultants – David Gluckman and Hugh Reade Seymour-Davies – hit on the idea of combining Irish whiskey, cream, and chocolate powder. More finessing followed, but the soon-to-be-world-famous flavour of Baileys was set. No one at the drinks company has ever worked out why people love drinking it at Christmas, and they've spent plenty of time and money trying to persuade drinkers to try Baileys throughout the rest of the year. But Baileys drinkers are stubborn – they like Baileys at Christmas, so a festive drink it is. It's also what gives this festive riff on an Espresso Martini its fudgy flavour. Boozy and sweet, this coffee-laced cocktail is a Yuletide treat.

50ml / 1¾fl oz vanilla vodka
25ml / 1fl oz coffee liqueur
25ml / 1fl oz hot, freshly brewed espresso
25ml / 1fl oz Baileys Irish Cream Liqueur
Cocoa powder, to garnish

1. Put a coupe glass in the freezer to chill for 5–10 minutes.

2. Half-fill a cocktail shaker with ice and pour in the vanilla vodka, coffee liqueur, espresso, and Baileys. Seal, then shake together for 30 seconds or until the tin is frosty.

3. Strain the cocktail into the chilled glass. Dust with a little cocoa powder to garnish and serve.

Christmas in New York

Serves 1

The Rockefeller Center Christmas tree. Ice skating in Central Park. Seeing the window displays on Fifth Avenue. And meeting Santa at Macy's. Christmas in New York is iconic. It's the stuff that dreams and holiday movies are made of. The vibe in the Big Apple is different in December; there are so many people thronging the streets that New York's famous fast pace slows down and the no-nonsense attitude melts a bit under all the tinsel and lights. Although not completely. New York is still New York underneath all the glitter and snow. But in the holiday season, you get to see a bit more of the city's warmth and the community spirit that ties New Yorkers together. Some of this is helped along by all the pop-up bars. In the markets, by the skating rinks, tucked into department stores – if there's space for a countertop, a few glasses, and some ice, a bar is squeezed in. You'll find all the usual Christmas suspects – mulled wine, spiced cider, hot chocolate – but when you're in NYC, it would be a shame not to try New York's most quintessential drink: the Manhattan. Invented in the 1860s by George Black at his bar on Broadway, it's a smooth, booze-forward cocktail with a silky texture. The combination of peppery rye whiskey with bittersweet vermouth is almost chocolatey. Add the Mulled Syrup (see page 18) in this version, and you get a delicately festive drink.

- 60ml / 2fl oz rye whiskey
- 25ml / 1fl oz sweet vermouth
- 8ml / ¼fl oz Mulled Syrup (see page 18)
- 3 dashes of Angostura bitters
- Maraschino cherry, to garnish

1. Put a Nick & Nora glass in the freezer to chill for 5–10 minutes.

2. Fill a mixing glass with ice. Pour in the whiskey, sweet vermouth, and Mulled Syrup. Dash in the Angostura bitters. Stir until well chilled – around 1 minute.

3. Strain the cocktail into the chilled glass. Drop in a maraschino cherry to garnish and serve.

Santa's Sidecar

Serves 1

Christmas is a sugary time of year. From candy canes, cakes, and cookies to gift boxes filled with chocolates, everything is a bit sweeter during the holidays. It's a season when drinks I wouldn't normally even *think* about sipping start creeping onto my bar cart, like butterscotch schnapps. At any other time of the year, I'd feel a bit embarrassed to order it. But at Christmas? When I've had cinnamon bun French toast for breakfast and swapped my morning coffee for a gingerbread-spiced hot chocolate laden with marshmallows and whipped cream? It's just part of the sweet-toothed fun. Flavoured schnapps have a very 1980s vibe. They hark back to a time when cocktail menus leaned sweet, fruity, and neon-bright. That might make you think you can't do anything too serious with them, but stir butterscotch schnapps into a Sidecar and you get a bright, crisp cocktail that is a beautiful balance of sticky and sharp. Classically, a Sidecar is a mix of cognac, triple sec, and lemon juice. Adding the butterscotch folds in a toffee twist of sweetness that's prevented from becoming too tooth-achingly syrupy by the fresh citrus. If you don't normally like sweet cocktails but all the Christmas treats are working their magic on you, then this is the holiday cocktail for you.

45ml / 1½fl oz French brandy
15ml / ½fl oz Cointreau
15ml / ½fl oz butterscotch schnapps
15ml / ½fl oz fresh lemon juice
Lemon twist, to garnish

1. Place a small coupe glass in the freezer to chill for 5–10 minutes.

2. Pour the brandy, Cointreau, butterscotch schnapps, and lemon juice into a cocktail shaker. Half-fill the tin with ice, seal, then shake for 15–30 seconds or until the tin is frosty.

3. Fine-strain the cocktail into the chilled glass. Take your lemon twist and twist it over the drink to express some of the oils, then drop it into the glass and serve.

St Louis-style Whiskey Punch

Serves 1

In 1966 a new midwinter festival was born. Kwanzaa was devised by Dr Maulana Karenga, a professor, activist, and author who wanted to create a non-religious celebration for Black Americans to honour their African roots. The year before, the Watts Riots tore through Los Angeles, sparked by an instance of race-related police brutality by the LAPD. In response, Dr Karenga created a community festival to celebrate African-American heritage and culture. Today, Kwanzaa – the name drawn from the Swahili phrase *matunda ya kwanza*, meaning 'first fruits' – is celebrated by the African diaspora around the world. From 26 December to 1 January, people come together to revere the seven principles of Kwanzaa with ceremonies, storytelling, poetry, dancing, music, and feasts. Mixing a cocktail created by the first Black American to publish a cocktail book, Tom Bullock, feels like fitting way to honour the occasion. Bullock's 1917 book *The Ideal Bartender* was dedicated 'To those who enjoy snug club rooms, that they may learn the art of preparing for themselves what is good.' Bullock spent 25 years mixing cocktails in Kentucky club houses, famous for his whiskey drinks. His St Louis-style Whiskey Punch is honeyed, lush, and rich. There's a trace of toffee sweetness brightened by a kick of fresh lemon.

- 45ml / 1½fl oz rye whiskey
- 15ml / ½fl oz sweet vermouth
- 15ml / ½fl oz Pineapple Syrup (see page 20)
- 15ml / ½fl oz fresh lemon juice
- Lemon twist, to garnish

1. Place a coupe glass into the freezer to chill for 5–10 minutes.

2. Pour the whiskey, sweet vermouth, Pineapple Syrup, and lemon juice into a cocktail shaker. Half-fill the tin with ice, seal, then shake for 15–30 seconds or until the tin is frosty.

3. Fine-strain the cocktail into the chilled glass. Twist the lemon twist over the drink, then drop it into the glass and serve.

Red & Green Heart

Serves 1

One way to check if your heart is two sizes too small is to see how you feel about Christmas.* (*Not to be interpreted as medical advice.) Do you love the festive season? Do you love it beyond all reason? Does it make you want to cheer? Is it your favourite time of year? Could you celebrate it in the sun? On a beach, would it still be fun? Could you party in the snow? If there were blizzards, would you still go? Do you like to spread festive joy? Does Christmas come with lots of toys? If that sounds a lot like you, then we should have a drink or two. Especially if the drink is this lurid green twist on a Margarita that was inspired by Dr Seuss's most famously unfestive Christmas character, The Grinch. It's sweetened with Midori, a melon-scented liqueur that gives the cocktail its neon-bright colour. The lush, musky flavour of the Midori is crisply paired with fresh lemon juice, a tropical splash of Pineapple Syrup (see page 20), and a punch of heat from the tequila. It will fill you with festive warmth from the inside out and is an easier way to feel the holiday joy than having your heart suddenly grow three sizes in one day.

45ml / 1½fl oz silver tequila
25ml / 1fl oz Midori liqueur
15ml / ½fl oz fresh lemon juice
10ml / ½fl oz Pineapple Syrup (see page 20)
Maraschino cherry, to garnish

1. Place a Nick & Nora glass in the freezer to chill for 5–10 minutes.

2. Pour the tequila, Midori, lemon juice, and Pineapple Syrup into a cocktail shaker. Half-fill the tin with ice, seal, then shake for 15–30 seconds or until the tin is frosty.

3. Double-strain the cocktail into the chilled glass. Drop the maraschino cherry (heart) into the glass or add it to a cocktail pick and serve.

Baddest Santa

Serves 1

One of the trickier Christmas movies to watch with family is 2003's *Bad Santa*. This holiday flick combines a booze-sodden Santa Claus with a lonely, socially maladjusted schoolkid, a furious safecracking elf, and a bartender with a Santa fetish. Yet somehow it delivers a story full of festive joy. I'm probably reaching a little to find a heartwarming moral in this cynically funny film. But, in its defence, most of the characters in the movie get the end they deserve. Admittedly, Billy Bob Thornton's character, the eponymous Bad Santa, does end up escaping justice, but as the film's anti-hero, he gets a pass. In tribute to the baddest of Santas, I created this smoky cocktail. It's based on a New York Sour, which is normally made with bourbon. This version uses a mix of mezcal and silver tequila as the base. The mezcal gives the drink a funky, earthy flavour with a hefty dose of ash. Shaken into a sour, it's tart and tangy with a sleazy, dive-bar vibe. The fluffy, white foam top is stained with red wine, which looks a little like drops of blood. The kind that might end up in a department-store Santa's beard, should he get into a bar fight.

- 30ml / 1fl oz mezcal
- 30ml / 1fl oz reposado tequila
- 30ml / 1fl oz fresh lemon juice
- 15ml / ½fl oz Simple Syrup (see page 18)
- 15ml / ½fl oz egg whites or aquafaba
- 8ml / ¼fl oz fruity red wine, like a Rioja or Shiraz

1. Pour the mezcal, tequila, lemon juice, Simple Syrup, and egg whites or aquafaba into a cocktail shaker. Top up the tin with ice. Seal, then shake well until the tin is frosty.

2. Strain into a clean glass. Discard the ice, then return the drink to the cocktail shaker. Seal, then shake again until the tin feels light and foamy.

3. Add ice to a rocks glass. Strain the cocktail into the glass. Float the red wine on top by pouring it over the back of a bar spoon. Serve straight away.

Mrs Claus's Secret

Serves 1

The holidays can be a joyful time. But they can also be a bit hectic. And no one knows that more than Mrs Claus, the unsung hero of the North Pole. Maintaining a domestic calm behind the storm of toymaking and list-checking, Mrs Claus ensures all the boring, everyday tasks still get done while other people (*cough* Santa Claus *cough*) showboat their way through their one seasonal task of the year. Not everyone gets the praise they deserve. But once Saint Nick is in his sled, flying through the air with a sack full of gifts, Mrs Claus does get that most precious of things: time to herself. In a quiet moment on Christmas Eve, when everything is done – the house is ready, the food prepared, and the games and decorations all arranged – Mrs Claus can kick off her shoes, run a bubble bath or sit down by the fire, and pour herself a well-deserved drink. If you've been running yourself ragged with holiday prep, then follow Mrs Claus's example and treat yourself to 30 minutes' blissful peace with a cocktail that tastes like boozy caramel sauce. And raise a toast to the power behind the sleigh, Mrs Claus.

60ml / 2fl oz bourbon
25ml / 1fl oz butterscotch schnapps
25ml / 1fl oz sweet vermouth
Maraschino cherry, to garnish

1. Place a Nick & Nora glass in the freezer to chill for 5–10 minutes.

2. Pour the bourbon, butterscotch schnapps, and vermouth into a mixing glass. Add ice and stir for 30–45 seconds to chill.

3. Strain into the chilled glass. Drop in a maraschino cherry to garnish and serve.

Under the Mistletoe

Serves 1

The tradition of kissing under the mistletoe began with Tudor kissing boughs in sixteenth-century England. These were woven ash or willow boughs threaded with evergreens, including mistletoe. These boughs were hung in the entrance halls to great houses, and hosts would embrace their guests beneath them as they arrived. By the 1700s, couples passing beneath the bough would have to kiss and men would pick a mistletoe berry. Once all the berries were plucked, there were no more kisses to be had. A certain amount of impropriety occurred underneath the kissing boughs, and many households insisted on hanging them somewhere more visible. By the Victorian period, sprigs of mistletoe were decorated with ribbon and hung in ballrooms, ensuring as many couples as possible could waltz beneath and steal a kiss. A newly minted superstition held that if a young woman refused a kiss below the mistletoe, she wouldn't receive any marriage proposals for the next year. If you remain resolutely unkissed this Christmas, mix yourself this cocktail by way of consolation. The fruity, sweet-shop flavour of the Midori is cut with a sour bite of lime and a lick of heat from the rum. Crisp, sharp, and tangy, it's a surer bet than a sprig of mistletoe.

- 35ml / 1¼fl oz light rum
- 25ml / 1fl oz Midori liqueur
- 15ml / ½fl oz fresh lime juice
- 15ml / ½fl oz egg whites or aquafaba
- 8ml / ¼fl oz Simple Syrup (see page 18)
- Lime wheel and maraschino cherry on a pick, to garnish

1. Place a Nick & Nora glass in the freezer to chill for 5–10 minutes.

2. Pour the rum, Midori, lime juice, egg whites or aquafaba, and Simple Syrup into a cocktail shaker. Top up the tin with ice. Seal, then shake well until the tin is frosty.

3. Strain into a clean glass. Discard the ice, then return the drink to the tin. Seal, then shake again until the tin feels light and foamy.

4. Strain the drink into the chilled glass. Thread a lime wheel and cherry onto a pick and rest on the rim, then serve.

Cinnamon Roll Martini

Serves 1

Among the Christmas spices – nutmeg, allspice, cloves, and ginger – one spice is king: cinnamon. From November to January, we're drenched in its cozy, comforting scent. It's in cakes, candles, cookies, decorations, and desserts. Cinnamon has become so closely associated with midwinter that when a 2009 social study asked participants to rank favourite scents at different times of year, cinnamon was downvoted in the summer but was top of the charts as soon as winter hit. In drinks, cinnamon can be a bit tricky. The warm flavour can end up tasting peppery and harsh. The secret is to pair it with something creamy. This velvety dessert cocktail partners hot Fireball Cinnamon Whiskey Liqueur with Baileys Irish Cream to cool down some of the liqueur's spicy heat. A dash of Beer Syrup (see page 20) rounds out the cocktail and gives it a yeasty, bready flavour – just like a real cinnamon roll. It's a decadent drink with more of a boozy punch than normal for a dessert drink. Try it as part of a festive brunch alongside pancakes and bacon.

45ml / 1½fl oz bourbon
35ml / 1¼fl oz Beer Syrup (see page 20)
15ml / ½fl oz Baileys Irish Cream Liqueur
8ml / ¼fl oz Fireball Cinnamon Whiskey Liqueur
Ground cinnamon, to garnish

1. Place a Nick & Nora glass in the freezer to chill for 5–10 minutes.

2. Pour the bourbon, Beer Syrup, Baileys, and Fireball into a cocktail shaker. Top up the tin with ice. Seal, then shake well until the tin is frosty.

3. Fine-strain the cocktail into the chilled glass. Dust over a little cinnamon to garnish, then serve.

Nutcracker

Serves 1

The Nutcracker ballet has its origins in a German children's novel, *The Nutcracker and The Mouse King*. Like all good German fairytales, it's dark, violent, and grotesque. And while ballet is no stranger to bloodletting and tragic demises, Tchaikovsky wanted something a bit lighter for his Yuletide ballet. So he drew on a more family-friendly retelling of the story by Alexandre Dumas, *Père*, which played up the magic, toys, and parties and focused less on mutant, bloodthirsty mice. The premiere took place in St Petersburg's Mariinsky Theatre in December 1892. It wasn't a success. Reviews were lukewarm, and Tchaikovsky himself despaired of it, declaring it 'infinitely worse than *Sleeping Beauty*'. How little he knew. *The Nutcracker* is now one of the most-performed ballets in the world. Families pack out theatres to watch gingerbreadmen battle a battalion of mice and then swoon over the Sugar Plum Fairy's ball in the Land of Sweets. A cocktail inspired by *The Nutcracker* is obviously going to be sweet and nutty, which is why this drink is based around Frangelico. It's an Italian hazelnut liqueur with a gorgeous buttery flavour. Shaken with crème de cacao, cream, and bourbon, it makes a luscious cocktail that fans of Ferrero Rocher will love.

- 45ml / 1½fl oz bourbon
- 35ml / 1¼fl oz double cream
- 25ml / 1fl oz Frangelico liqueur
- 15ml / ½fl oz dark crème de cacao
- Cocoa powder, to garnish

1. Place a Nick & Nora glass in the freezer to chill for 5–10 minutes.

2. Pour the bourbon, cream, Frangelico, and dark crème de cacao into a cocktail shaker. Top up the tin with ice. Seal, then shake well until the tin is frosty.

3. Strain the cocktail into the chilled glass. Dust over a little cocoa powder to garnish, then serve.

Saint Nick

Serves 1

There's a tendency to think that, when it comes to Martinis, drier is better. But the first proto-Martini was wet – very, *very* wet – and I think it was better for it. Wetness in a Martini refers to how much vermouth there is in the drink compared to gin (or vodka). Three parts gin to one part dry vermouth is the starting point for a Dry Martini. But the original drink that all modern Martinis are based on was the Martinez, which was made with a 1:1 ratio of gin to sweet vermouth. Essentially, it was a Gin Manhattan. The equal weighting of gin and sweet vermouth means you get a satisfying mix of juniper and bitter herbs in the glass. This festive version swaps the vermouth for Harveys Bristol Cream Sherry. Amber-coloured, mellow, and fragrant, Harveys is made by blending together fino, amontillado, olorosos, and Pedro Ximénez sherries. It's plump with dried fruit and spice and is very popular at Christmas in Britain – especially served chilled with a warm mince pie on the side. Stirred with gin and a dash of apricot brandy, it makes an elegant, silky cocktail with a lemony twist. This cocktail is at its best when it's served very cold, so make sure you stir it with plenty of ice and chill the serving glass in advance.

45ml / 1½fl oz London Dry Gin
45ml / 1½fl oz Harveys Bristol Cream Sherry
15ml / ½fl oz apricot brandy
Maraschino cherry and lemon twist, to garnish

1. Put a Nick & Nora glass into the freezer to chill for 5–10 minutes.

2. Fill a mixing glass with ice. Pour in the gin, sherry, and apricot brandy. Stir until well chilled – around 1 minute.

3. Strain the cocktail into the chilled glass. Drop in a maraschino cherry. Take your lemon twist and twist it over the drink to express some of the oils, then drop it into the glass and serve.

Mulled Spritz

Serves 1

In Venice, the spiritual home of the Aperol Spritz, Christmas begins on 8 December – the Feast of the Immaculate Conception (of Mary, rather than Jesus). As well as going to Mass, it's the day Italians traditionally put up their festive decorations, nativity cribs, and Christmas trees. In Venice, that often means digging out a box of handmade glass baubles from Murano. Elegantly swirled and dotted with gem-bright colours, these baubles are a credit to St Nicholas, who manages to fit in being the patron saint of glassblowers, as well as delivering presents to all the good girls and boys. Once the Christmas tree is set up, the first of many festive feasts can take place. It's a family affair and dishes like *bigoli in salsa* (pasta with onions and anchovies) or *risotto al radicchio* might be on the menu. If you can't make it to Venice to see the decorated trees in the piazzas and the cribs in the shopfronts, bring the city's spirit to your home by making a Christmas-themed Spritz. It's sweetened with a splash of Mulled Syrup (see page 18), which gives the bittersweet flavour of the Aperol a seasonally spicy lift.

60ml / 2fl oz Aperol
15ml / ¼fl oz Mulled Syrup (see page 18)
90ml / 3fl oz dry prosecco, chilled
35ml / 1¼fl oz soda water, chilled
Orange wheel, to garnish

1. Fill a copa or wine glass with ice. Pour in the Aperol and Mulled Syrup. Stir together for 30 seconds to chill them.

2. Top the glass up with the prosecco, then the soda water. Stir briefly, then tuck an orange wheel into the glass to garnish. Serve straight away.

MAKE YOUR OWN PEAR PURÉE

You can buy readymade pear purée, but it's easy to make your own. Peel, core, and roughly chop 2 pears. Place in a steamer basket and set over a pan of simmering water for 8–10 minutes or until the pears are very soft. Scoop the pears into a blender and add 3 tablespoons water. Blend for 1–2 minutes until smooth. Press it through a sieve for added smoothness. Store in the fridge for up to 3 days.

Pear & Ginger Bellini

Serves 4

The New Year doesn't always begin on 1 January. Depending on where you are in the world, the New Year might start in late January/early February (Lunar New Year), March (Balinese Nyepi), April (Sinhala and Tamil New Year), September (Coptic New Year), or throughout the autumn (Jewish Rosh Hashanah). Even in Western Europe, 31 December wasn't always New Year's Eve. When the Julian calendar kept track of time, the New Year might take place on 25 March or 25 December. It was only when the Gregorian calendar was introduced that the turn of the year was fixed in place at the end of December. The 31 December is now a big-enough event to mean fireworks and parties follow the midnight chimes around the world. And big parties demand fabulous drinks. This crowd-pleasing, sparkling cocktail is fruity and fizzy with a sneaky kiss of heat. The pear purée combined with the Gingerbread Syrup (see page 19) gives it a luscious sweetness, while the applejack brandy means there's just enough booze in it to keep things interesting. Depending on your perspective, the swirl of edible glitter is either over the top and ridiculous or the dash of glamour required of drinks on New Year's Eve.

120g / 4¼oz pear purée
40ml / 1½fl oz applejack brandy
40ml / 1½fl oz Gingerbread Syrup (see page 19)
480ml / 17fl oz dry prosecco, chilled
Edible glitter flakes, to garnish

1. Spoon the pear purée into four flute glasses. Add 2 teaspoons of applejack brandy and 2 teaspoons of Gingerbread Syrup to each glass. Gently stir to mix using a bar spoon.

2. Top up each glass with the chilled prosecco and gently stir again to mix.

3. Drop a pinch of edible glitter flakes into each glass and serve immediately.

Snowflake

Serves 1

The drinking public have done the Snowball dirty. A crisp and light combination of Advocaat, brandy, lime cordial, and sparkling lemonade, it's believed to have been invented in Britain in the 1940s or 1950s – although the 1950s seem more likely, with the lifting of rations. It didn't really become popular until the 1970s, when suddenly Christmas wasn't Christmas without an Advocaat and lemonade. The cocktail dominated the Yuletide drinking scene in Britain like no other. But then the 1980s arrived, with neon-hued Martinis and fruit-based cocktails. Overnight, the Dutch egg liqueur was relegated to the back of the drinks cupboard – only dusted off once a year for an auntie or grandma who still liked a Christmas Snowball. It's a much better cocktail than its naff reputation suggests, but if you're not convinced, try making it with Champagne. Because Champagne improves everything. The satin-soft, custardy liqueur is lifted by the Champagne's fizz and sharpened by the fresh lime juice. It's lively, luxurious, and a lot of fun.

75ml / 3fl oz Advocaat
30ml / 2fl oz fino sherry
15ml / ¼fl oz fresh lime juice
50ml / 1¾fl oz brut Champagne, chilled
Cocoa powder, to garnish

1. Place the flute glass in the freezer to chill for 5–10 minutes.

2. Pour the Advocaat, sherry, and lime juice into a cocktail shaker. Top it up with ice, seal, then shake until the tin is frosty – around 30 seconds.

3. Take the glass out of the freezer and pour in the chilled Champagne. Strain the Advocaat mix into the glass, letting it slink through the Champagne.

4. Dust over a little cocoa powder and serve.

Out of Office

Serves 1

Once you're a grownup and the thrill of waking up to a stocking full of presents has lost its magic, there's no better feeling than clocking off work for Christmas. Being British, most of my jobs have marked the start of the Christmas break with an early finish and a trip to the pub for a pint. Even when I worked on Christmas Day as a barmaid, the moment the last of the holiday drinkers were out the door, all the staff had a drink poured for them by the landlord so we could toast the season (and to help jolly us along as we cleaned). Capturing that fizzing sense of anticipation and release in a cocktail requires Champagne. The tiny bubbles bursting in the glass are shorthand for fun. A classic Champagne cocktail is made with cognac and is a reliable go-to for celebrations, but in this version I've swapped it for rye whiskey. The caramel spiciness of the rye gives this drink a wilder edge. It has a celebratory kick and plenty of punch. Put on your out-of-office, lock the office door, and raise a glass. The holidays are here.

1 Demerara sugar cube
3 dashes of Angostura bitters
25ml / 1fl oz rye whiskey, chilled
120ml / 4fl oz brut Champagne, chilled
Orange twist, to garnish

1. Place the sugar cube on a bar spoon. Dash the Angostura bitters over the top to coat the sugar cube and let it soak in. Drop it into a flute glass.

2. Pour the chilled whiskey into the glass. Use the bar spoon to stir them together to dissolve the sugar cube. Top up the glass with the chilled Champagne.

3. Take the orange twist and twist it over the glass to express the oils. Drop it into the glass or rest on the rim and serve.

Christmas Kiss

Serves 2

Is there anything sweeter than a kiss at Christmas? Whether it's a secret smooch underneath the mistletoe, a cheeky snog at the office Christmas party, or a loving peck on the cheek from your grandmother who's delighted to get a set of bath salts from you *yet again*, nothing will put a glow in your cheeks quite like a Christmas kiss. Sometimes, when it's romantic, making that kiss happen needs a little bit of Dutch courage. Which is where this silken cream cocktail comes in. I designed it as a generously measured shooter, but it's good enough to sip if you want to take time to build up a connection with the object of your festive desires. Chocolatey, with a little touch of heat that will linger on your lips, it's a drink that is designed to be shared. To shoot it, you'll need two 60ml / 2fl oz shot glasses. Otherwise, use small coupe or Nick & Nora glasses for sipping (make sure they're chilled). Now go find the mistletoe and make those festive feelings known.

- 30ml / 1fl oz Fireball Cinnamon Whisky Liqueur, chilled
- 30ml / 1fl oz dark crème de cacao, chilled
- 50ml / 1¾fl oz Baileys Irish Cream Liqueur, chilled

1. Take two large, chilled shot glasses and divide the chilled Fireball between them.

2. Pour 15ml / ¼fl oz chilled dark crème de cacao into each glass, then top them up with 25ml / 1fl oz chilled Baileys each. Serve straight away.

Tipsy Snowman

Serves 2

Everybody loves building a snowman, even though we know they won't last. It's the downside to using snow as your modelling clay. As soon as the sun comes out, the snow melts away and the cheery snow pal who was guarding your garden is gone. In the 1982 animated film *The Snowman*, we all knew that the magical snowman who danced, clowned about, and flew to the North Pole to visit Father Christmas wouldn't last forever, but it is still heartbreaking every time he melts. At least The Snowman has a good time with Santa at his Christmas Party, because St Nick puts on quite a spread. There's plenty to eat at his holiday party, alongside beer, wine, lemonade, and even cups of tea. All that's missing is the cocktails, which is where these minty cream drinks come in. Satin-smooth and rich with a refreshing peppermint bite, they're perfect as a dessert drink at the end of a festive meal. Use small, chilled coupes or martini glasses or 60ml / 2fl oz shot glasses to serve them, depending on whether you want to sip or shoot them.

50ml / 1¾fl oz Baileys Irish Cream Liqueur, chilled

50ml / 1¾fl oz peppermint schnapps, chilled

1. Take two large, chilled shot glasses and divide the chilled Baileys between them. Then pour 25ml / 1fl oz peppermint schnapps into each glass. Serve straight away.

Small Town Hottie

Serves 1

Every Christmas I regret that I don't have a small town to go home to, where a rugged yet sensitive man in a plaid shirt can welcome me back and cure me of my big-city notions with his homely, country ways. I do go on a few trips to small towns and villages throughout December in case there are any handsome Christmas tree farmers, Christmas cookie bakers, Christmas card designers, or straight-up handymen looking for a burnt-out, career-girl wife. But so far, no dice. In the absence of a charming, wholesome, and surprisingly well-muscled man, this Yuletide twist on a Hot Toddy will put a pink glow in your cheeks. It has blended Scotch whisky at its heart for heat and a buttery hit of citrus and spice. The Gingerbread Syrup (see page 19) is sweet and warming, while the fresh lemon juice cuts through the booze. I always think a Hot Toddy can cure the common cold. This version might also mend a jaded heart.

- 75ml / 3fl oz freshly boiled water
- 35ml / 1¼fl oz Scotch whisky
- 20ml / ¾fl oz Gingerbread Syrup (see page 19)
- 8ml / ¼fl oz fresh lemon juice
- Lemon wheel and cloves, to garnish

1. Let the boiled water cool in a heatproof pitcher for 1–2 minutes.

2. Pour the whisky, Gingerbread Syrup, and lemon juice into a heatproof glass or mug.

3. Stud the lemon wheel with 3–4 cloves and drop into or add to the rim of the glass.

4. Pour the hot water into the glass and gently stir to mix. Serve straight away.

Honey Buttered Rum

Serves 1

Originally a medicinal drink, Hot Buttered Rum was prescribed as a cure for sore throats and sleeplessness in sixteenth-century England. A pat of butter would be whisked into hot rum sweetened with sugar and winter spices, then handed to the lucky patient. With such a mix of expensive ingredients, this wasn't a cure for the common man. In the depths of winter, when the palaces were frosted inside and out, it would have been a very soothing drink and might even have put Henry VIII in a good mood (depending where he was with his wives). This version is made with spiced honey butter. The amber sweetness of the honey melts into the drink with the butter, giving it a lavish texture and rich flavour. It's deeply comforting and has an old-fashioned feel. Every sip conjures up flashes of dark, low-ceilinged taverns with roaring fires and pewter tankards hanging by the bar. It's a great drink to mix after a cold winter walk. Or take it in a keep cup to your local Christmas market.

FOR THE SPICED HONEY BUTTER
- 125g / 4¼oz lightly salted butter, softened
- 75ml / 3fl oz honey
- 55g / 2oz soft brown sugar
- ½ tsp ground cinnamon
- ½ tsp ground ginger
- ½ tsp allspice
- ¼ tsp ground cloves
- Grating of nutmeg

FOR ONE SERVING
- 25ml / 1fl oz dark rum
- 125ml / 4¼fl oz freshly boiled water
- 1–2 tbsp double cream and nutmeg, to garnish

1. To make the honey butter, scoop the softened butter into a bowl and add the honey and soft brown sugar. Beat together with electric beaters or a wooden spoon until smoothly combined. Add the spices and beat again. Scoop into a tub, seal, then store in the fridge. The butter will keep for 3–4 weeks.

2. To make a glass of Honey Buttered Rum, scoop 2 tablespoons of the spiced butter into a heatproof mug or glass. Add the dark rum and top up with the freshly boiled water. Stir well to mix. Pour the cream over a bar spoon to float it on top of the rum. Grate over a little nutmeg (don't skip this) and serve straight away.

White Christmas

Serves 1

Every year in the UK, people bet on whether it will be a white Christmas. To count as a white Christmas, a single snowflake must be seen falling on 25 December by either a Met Office observer or a Met Office automated weather station. (The Met Office is the UK's national weather service.) It happens less often than you'd think. Especially if you grew up with Dickensian images of London coated in snow and ice. Since 1960, just 5 per cent of the network has reported a white Christmas for only half of the years. There have only been four years when enough snow has fallen to cover the ground – 1981, 1995, 2009, and 2010 – but even then, that was reported by just 40 per cent of the stations. So, if you're travelling to the UK in the hopes of experiencing a snowy Christmas, be prepared to find it cold and wet rather than romantically frosty. Of course, it is still chilly, so you'd be justified in making a warming, booze-spiked hot chocolate to help defrost your fingers and toes. This moreish, white hot chocolate is vanilla-rich and sumptuous. If you want to make a family-friendly version, leave out the RumChata and add a generous pinch of ground cardamom to the milk with the vanilla extract.

60g / 2oz white chocolate
250ml / 8½fl oz full-fat milk
½ tsp vanilla extract
45ml / 1½fl oz RumChata Cream Liqueur
Whipped cream and mini marshmallows, to serve

1. Coarsely grate the white chocolate and add it to a small pan. Pour in the milk and add the vanilla extract. Set the pan over a medium heat and gently warm, stirring, until the chocolate has melted and is smoothly combined.

2. Pour the RumChata into a heatproof glass or mug. Pour in the white hot chocolate. Top with whipped cream and mini marshmallows and serve straight away.

Christmapolitan

Serves 6

No cocktail says girls' night in more than a Cosmopolitan. A tart and tangy mixture of vodka, cranberry, lime, and Cointreau, it started off as a party drink in gay bars in 1970s San Francisco. In the 1990s, it got a second wind when Carrie, Samantha, Miranda, and Charlotte made it their drink of choice in *Sex and the City*. Over the years, there have been plenty of variations mixed. This Christmas version swaps dry Cointreau for a more festive mix of Velvet Falernum and Tuaca. Both the Falernum and Tuaca are infused with spices – vanilla in the Tuaca and cloves in the Falernum. They also include lime and orange zests and a creamy note of almonds – all flavours that are richly associated with Christmas. The result is a tart, dry cocktail that's refreshingly fruity with a zingy nip of spice. A little bit flirty and a lot of fun, it's a great drink to split with your gal pals while you spill the office Christmas party gossip.

360ml / 12fl oz vodka
75ml / 2½fl oz Velvet Falernum Liqueur
75ml / 2½fl oz Tuaca Liqueur
150ml / 5¼fl oz fresh lime juice
150ml / 5¼fl oz cranberry juice drink
50ml / 2fl oz Simple Syrup (see page 18)
12 dashes of orange bitters
Lime wheels, to garnish

1. Pour the vodka, Velvet Falernum, Tuaca, fresh lime juice, cranberry juice, and Simple Syrup into a pitcher. Dash in the orange bitters and stir well to mix. Chill in the fridge for 4–6 hours. You can pour the mix into a bottle, seal it, then store in the fridge for up to 3 days.

2. To serve, fill six rocks glasses with ice. Pour in the Christmapolitan mix. Garnish the glasses with lime wheels and serve.

Sangría Navideña

Serves 6

If you like a spiced wine punch at Christmas but don't love Mulled Wine, you should try mixing up a pitcher of Sangría. Fruit-filled wine punches have been popular in Europe for centuries. In Spain, they've drunk Limonada de León – a mix of red wine, lemon juice, sugar, and cinnamon – since the Middle Ages. In the eighteenth century a similar punch started being mixed by British colonists in the West Indies, except they replaced the red wine with Madeira and called it Sangaree. It's not hard to imagine a contingent of Spanish sailors introducing the basic recipe for Limonada to the British and then taking the new name back home with them. Sangría ended up becoming embedded in Spanish culture, although these days it's mostly drunk by tourists (those in the know order a Tinto de Verano). At its most simple, Sangría is a cocktail of red wine, brandy, fruit juice, and chopped fruit. This refreshingly fizzy Christmas version uses pineapple juice to give the drink some tropical sweetness and ginger ale for the bubbles. A mixture of brandy and passionfruit liqueur backs up the pineapple and gives the Sangría some oomph. It's crisp and tangy with lots of juicy fruit. A great pick for parties or Christmas in warmer climes.

- 2 lemons
- 2 oranges
- 120ml / 4¼fl oz Spanish brandy
- 60ml / 2fl oz passionfruit liqueur
- 500ml / 17½fl oz red wine, such as Garnacha, Tempranillo, or Rioja
- 250ml / 8¾fl oz pineapple juice
- 750ml / 1⅓ pints ginger ale, chilled

1. Slice the lemons and oranges into rounds and scoop them into a large pitcher. Pour in the brandy, passionfruit liqueur, and red wine. Gently stir to mix, then set aside for 2–3 hours to steep.

2. When you're ready to serve the Sangría, add 2 cupfuls of ice to the pitcher. Pour in the pineapple juice and stir well to mix. Top up the pitcher with the chilled ginger ale. Serve the Sangría in ice-filled rocks glasses.

Christmas on the Beach

Serves 6

In Australia you're more likely to get sandmen than snowmen, because an Aussie Christmas is spent on the beach. People flock to the seaside early, and by mid-morning most of the shore is filled with revellers, some of them wearing red bathers and Santa hats, ready for a Christmas Day dip. It's a longer, less-bracing affair than Christmas sea swims in Europe. And unlike their frozen cousins in the Northern Hemisphere, Australian beachgoers can actually stick around and enjoy a few hours in the warm sunshine. If you're shivering in the cold and long for some Aussie beach party vibes as part of your Christmas, mix up this festive twist on a classic 80's cocktail – Sex on the Beach. The original version is a mix of vodka, orange juice, peach schnapps, cranberry juice, and Chambord. This one swaps in pomegranate juice and uses tangy Cranberry Syrup (see page 19) to sweeten the mix. It's a fresh, fun, and crowd-pleasing cocktail that conjures up festive seaside picnics and warm, sunny Yuletide days.

- 300ml / 10½fl oz pomegranate juice drink
- 300ml / 10½fl oz fresh orange juice
- 150ml / 5¼fl oz vodka
- 150ml / 5¼fl oz crème de pêche
- 60ml / 2fl oz Cranberry Syrup (see page 19)
- 60ml / 2fl oz fresh lime juice
- Orange wheels and maraschino cherries, to garnish

1. Pour the pomegranate and orange juices into a large pitcher. Add the vodka, crème de pêche, Cranberry Syrup, and lime juice. Stir to mix, then chill for 3–4 hours. You can pour the mix into bottles, seal them, then store in the fridge for up to 3 days, ready to pour.

2. To serve, fill six old fashioned glasses with crushed ice. Pour in the Christmas on the Beach mix.

3. Thread orange wheels and maraschino cherries onto picks, rest them on the glasses to garnish, and serve.

Eggnog

Serves 4

A riot at West Point Military Academy in New York State was once sparked by too much Eggnog. It was 1826, the year before alcohol was banned from the site. On Christmas Eve most of the cadets retired to their dormitories, but those in the North Barracks were determined to see in Christmas with a drink, as they'd been smuggling in whisky, brandy, rum, wine, and beer for weeks. The party began quietly, but as the numbers swelled, the celebrations grew noisier, and by 4am they were loud enough to wake up a faculty member, Captain Hitchcock, who went to investigate. Finding 13 drunken cadets mixing drinks in one room, he read them the literal Riot Act, which led to them actually rioting. Dozens of Christmas-spirit-fuelled men ran through the halls brandishing weapons and hurling sticks and stones. Nearly one-third of the Academy's cadets were involved in the mêlée, which quickly became known as the Eggnog Riot. All of this is to say: don't drink too much Eggnog at Christmas. Even if it is delicious. You don't want to land in Eggnog jail.

2 medium eggs
60ml / 2fl oz Simple Syrup (see page 18)
100ml / 3½fl oz French brandy
200ml / 7fl oz double cream
300ml / 10fl oz full-fat milk
Nutmeg, to garnish

1. Place four rocks glasses in the freezer to chill for 5–10 minutes.

2. Separate the eggs into two clean, non-plastic bowls. Add the Simple Syrup and brandy to the egg yolks and whisk them together until they're smoothly combined. Pour in the double cream and milk and whisk well to combine.

3. In the other bowl, use electric beaters to whip the egg whites until they're light, fluffy, and soft peaks form. Use a flexible spatula to fold the egg whites through the egg yolks, cream, milk, and brandy mixture.

4. Ladle the Eggnog into the chilled glasses. Grate (essential!) fresh nutmeg over and serve.

North Pole Martini

Serves 6–10

Santa Claus moved to the North Pole in the 1860s, thanks to an American cartoonist. Thomas Nast regularly drew Christmas scenes for *Harper's Weekly* magazine, and in 1866 his vignette of Santa going about his work included the location Santaclaussville, N.P, which stood for 'North Pole'. Distant, isolated, and naturally associated in the public mind with snow, reindeers, and wonder, it was the perfect setting for Nast's magically industrious Santa. A busy man, Santa no doubt plans ahead at Christmas – especially for entertaining. I wouldn't be surprised to find a bottle of batched Martini tucked away in an ice cave, ready to pour when guests drop in. Stashing a bottle of Martini in your freezer is handy prep for spontaneous parties, or for simply making sure you have an ice-cold cocktail ready to pour on days when Christmas gets a bit hectic. Fresh from the freezer, this cocktail is gorgeously viscous and slippery. The flavour rests on the quality of the gin. I prefer a good London Dry Gin, for the piney hit of juniper. If you prefer a more botanical gin, use that. Make sure you don't skimp on the quality of the dry vermouth, either. Noilly Prat Original Dry Vermouth, with its aromatic mix of chamomile, elderflower, and bitter orange, is a great all-rounder.

- 125ml / 4¼fl oz dry vermouth
- 125ml / 4¼fl oz filtered water
- 8 dashes of orange bitters
- 450ml / 15¼fl oz London Dry Gin
- Lemon twist, to garnish

1. Sterilize a glass bottle following the method on page 17. Let it cool.

2. Pour the vermouth and water into the bottle. Add the bitters and swirl to mix, then top up with the gin. Seal and shake well. Place in the freezer for at least 6 hours. It will keep for months in the freezer.

3. To serve, chill a martini glass in the freezer for 15 minutes. Take the Martini out of the freezer and let it sit at room temperature for 1–2 minutes, then pour 75–100ml / 3–4fl oz into the cold glass. Twist the lemon twist over the Martini to express the oils, then drop into the glass and serve.

Frozen Cranberry Daiquiris

Serves 6

The North American cranberry harvest begins in mid-September and lasts until early November, giving cranberry lovers plenty of time to make jars of sauce to go with their Christmas (and Thanksgiving) roasts. Bright, tart, and a little astringent, cranberries are almost impossible to eat on their own. But they make a great ingredient. Their mouth-drying sourness is ideal for balancing sweet and herbal flavours. They're also a good foil for alcohol, which makes them a must-use in Yuletide cocktails. This Frozen Daiquiri uses a combination of cranberry juice and Cranberry Syrup (see page 19) to pump up the tangy, berry flavours. The amount of syrup probably seems mad, but freezing the mixture reduces its sweetness. Frozen food always needs more sugar than you'd expect to taste sweet. Blitzed in a blender, the rum-heavy mix turns into a grownup slushy that would be perfect for Christmas by the pool (real or imaginary).

400ml / 14fl oz light rum
350ml / 12¼fl oz Cranberry Syrup (see page 19)
75ml / 2½fl oz fresh lime juice
150ml / 5¼fl oz cranberry juice drink
Lime wheels and fresh cranberries, to garnish

1. Pour the rum, Cranberry Syrup, lime juice, and cranberry juice drink into a freezerproof container and stir to mix. Seal and freeze for at least 24 hours. The mix will keep well for up to 1 week.

2. When you're ready to serve the Daiquiris, place six coupes in the freezer for 5–10 minutes to chill.

3. Scoop the frozen rum mixture into a blender and add 2 cups of ice. Blitz until slushy, then pour into the coupes. Garnish the glasses with lime wheels and fresh cranberries. Serve straight away.

Christmas Star

Serves 4

Vibrant red-and-green poinsettias are a familiar sight at Christmas. They're native to Mexico, where they bloom from mid-December. There's a legend that their midwinter colours are down to a Christmas miracle. A young girl named Pepita was on her way to church on Christmas Eve when she realized she had no offering to give the newborn Jesus. Her brother consoled her that any gift, no matter how small, would be appreciated. So she gathered a bouquet of roadside weeds. When she laid them at the base of the altar, they burst into lush red flowers, earning poinsettias the nickname *la flor de Nochebuena*, or 'the Christmas Eve flower'. They're also known as Christmas stars, after the Bethlehem star, and I've adopted that name for this pink-tinged drink. The colour comes from a dash of tangy Cranberry Syrup (see page 19) and crème de noyaux, a rosy-red French liqueur with a rich, marzipan flavour. If you can't find crème de noyaux in your local bottle shop, swap in amaretto or Frangelico. You'll lose the colour but keep the nutty lushness that gives this Champagne cocktail its biscuit-and-berries flavour.

40ml / 2fl oz crème de noyaux
40ml / 2fl oz Cranberry Syrup (see page 19)
480ml / 16fl oz brut Champagne, chilled

1. Pour the crème de noyaux and Cranberry Syrup evenly between four flute glasses.

2. Top up each glass with the chilled Champagne and serve.

Home for the Holidays

Serves 6

The second-best feeling in the world – after signing off from work for Christmas (see page 91, for the cocktail to go with that feeling) – is arriving home for the holidays. Getting home is often a battle. For a long time, I had to take the train with every other holiday traveller in London. We'd all squeeze into the carriages, playing Tetris with our suitcases, bags of presents, and bottles of wine. Whatever seasonal goodwill people had on their way to the station evaporated pretty quickly as the train lurched along the tracks, weighed down by the sheer number of passengers determined to spend Christmas with their families. But the mood would pick up as people got off at stops along the way and were greeted on the platforms with hugs and kisses. By the time my station drew near, I'd have a seat, space to stretch my legs, and I'd be thinking fondly of the roaring fire and homecooked meal that was waiting for me. The first drink I have with my mum and dad is always a cup of tea. Something alcoholic follows swiftly on after that. This orchard twist on a Mimosa is designed to be poured the second all my sisters and I are home. It's an easy sipper that's not tricky to make and has a cozy, welcoming flavour. It tastes like apple pie and family gossip.

- 1 egg white (or 30ml / 2tbsp aquafaba)
- 1–2 tbsp soft brown sugar
- 180ml / 6¼fl oz applejack brandy, chilled
- 360ml / 12¼fl oz apple juice, chilled
- 540ml / 19¼fl oz brut Champagne, chilled

1. Add an egg white to a saucer and whisk it with a fork to loosen it. Tip the soft brown sugar onto a second saucer. Dip the rim of each glass in the egg white and then the sugar to coat. Chill the glasses in the fridge until you're ready to serve the drink.

2. Pour 30ml / 1fl oz applejack brandy into each chilled glass, then pour in 60ml / 2fl oz apple juice. Top up each glass with the chilled Champagne. Serve straight away.

Naughty & Nice Shots

Each serves 6

Try making a bottle of each of these shooters at your Christmas party and offer people the choice. I guarantee you 90 per cent of your guests will pick the Naughty Shot. And they will be wrong to do so – because it is awful. Genuinely, a terrible experience. And even though I've warned you and you may, in turn, warn *them*, partygoers will still pick Naughty because humans are contrary. The 'Naughty' mix of Fireball and tequila is peppery, punchy, and harsh. And that's before you add a dash of fiery hot sauce. Knocking back a shot of Naughty will make you pull a horrible face and gasp in shock. The Nice Shot, by contrast, is light, fresh, and creamy – a dream to drink. A silken blend of white chocolate and peppermint with a smooth, easy-sipping finish. But people will go Naughty, watch each other splutter their way through the drink, and then slap each other on the back. These shooters are best made the day before to give them plenty of time to chill. When doing shots, make sure there's plenty of food and water on hand to soak up the alcohol, and keep everyone hydrated.

FOR THE NAUGHTY SHOTS
- 120ml / 4fl oz Fireball Cinnamon Whisky Liqueur
- 120ml / 4fl oz reposado tequila
- Hot sauce, to serve

FOR THE NICE SHOTS
- 80ml / 2½fl oz white crème de cacao
- 80ml / 2½fl oz peppermint schnapps
- 40ml / 1½fl oz single cream

1. Sterilize two glass bottles following the method on page 17.

2. To make the Naughty Shots, pour the Fireball and tequila into a sterilized bottle. Seal and swirl to mix, then chill in the fridge for at least 6 hours (but ideally 24). It will keep for 3–4 days.

3. To make the Nice Shots, pour the white crème de cacao, peppermint schnapps, and cream into a sterilized bottle, then chill in the fridge for at least 6 hours (but ideally 24). It will keep in the fridge for 1–2 days.

4. To serve, let people choose their shot. Pour around 40ml / 1½fl oz into a shot glass. If they picked Naughty, add a couple dashes of hot sauce before handing it over.

Mulled Wine

Serves 8

Warm, spiced wine has been drunk across Europe since the Ancient Greeks prescribed it as a health tonic. They probably learned the technique from the Ancient Egyptians, who had at least 700 different types of infused wine to treat all kinds of ills. Doctors continued dishing out soothing cups of hot, sweet wine, well-flavoured with spices, until the late Medieval period. Eventually, it became more of a pleasure than a medicine. It has gone in and out of fashion, but has been growing in popularity more recently, ever since German-style Christmas markets began their midwinter takeover of town squares (or English-style markets, if you're in Germany). The secret to making Mulled Wine is to take your time. Don't boil it; let the wine gently steam over a low heat so the sugar melts and the spices leach their flavours. That way you get a Mull that's aromatic and warming but hasn't lost too much of the booze. If you have a slow cooker, you can use that to make really delicious Mulled Wine. Set it to low and let the wine, spices, and sugar warm for 4 hours, then add the port just before serving.

2 oranges
12 whole cloves
3 cinnamon sticks
20g / ¾oz fresh ginger
150g / 5¼oz granulated sugar
750ml / 1⅓ pints red wine, such as a Merlot or Malbec
250ml / 8½fl oz fresh orange juice
150ml / 5¼fl oz ruby port

1. Slice the oranges into rounds and push a few cloves into each. Place the orange slices into a large pan and add the cinnamon sticks. Thinly slice the ginger and drop into the pan. Tip in the sugar.

2. Pour in the wine and orange juice. Set the pan over a medium heat and warm until the wine is just steaming but not bubbling, stirring occasionally to dissolve the sugar.

3. When the wine is steaming hot, turn down the heat to low and cover the pan with a lid. Gently heat for 1 hour. After 1 hour, turn off the heat then pour in the port and stir to mix. Ladle into mugs or heatproof glasses to serve.

Baby Eggnog

Serves 1

If you ever thought that drinking custard sounded like a good idea, this is the mocktail for you. It's a zero-proof version of Eggnog that's creamy and decadent with a warm hint of spice, thanks to the nutmeg dusted on top. (This is essential – don't skip it!) It tastes like an old-fashioned English custard tart or a traditional rice pudding. It is an evolution of a drink that began with Medieval monks. In chilly England during the fourteenth century, people would warm up with a hot concoction of beer, milk, and spices called a posset. Monks, who never seemed to go short on luxury ingredients, began whisking eggs and dried figs into their drinks. Eventually, this custom spread to the manors and castles. By the seventeenth century, aristocrats were making their Eggnogs with fortified wines, like sherry, as a sign of their wealth. The drink travelled to America with the colonists, who subbed in Caribbean rum, as it was cheaper than imported European wines. When rum wasn't available, they used local whiskey or brandy instead. But you don't actually need the booze to make it taste nice. And now that we have central heating to warm our bones, we can drink our alcohol-free Eggnog over ice. It's still made with a whole raw egg, though, so please be mindful about who you serve it to (see page 16 for advice).

15ml / ¼fl oz Simple Syrup (see page 18)
½ tsp vanilla extract
50ml / 1¾fl oz double cream
65ml / 2¼fl oz full-fat milk
1 small egg
Nutmeg, to garnish

1. Pour the Simple Syrup, vanilla extract, cream, and milk into a cocktail shaker. Crack in the egg. Half-fill the tin with ice, seal, then shake for 15–30 seconds or until the tin is frosty.

2. Add a few ice cubes to a rocks glass, then fine-strain the Baby Eggnog into the glass. Grate over a little fresh nutmeg to serve.

Jingle Bell Fizz

Serves 6

A mocktail that's tangy and refreshing enough for adults, but not so dry that kids won't enjoy it, is a useful thing to have on hand during the Christmas party season. This hyper-quaffable, zero-proof fizz is a great pitcher drink for festive get-togethers. There's heat from the ginger beer, sweetness from the apple juice, and the fresh lime gives the cranberry a bit of zip. Best of all, it's really easy to make. So you have plenty of time to focus on fun things, like music, food, and what kind of Christmas jumper to wear. My Christmas jumper is bright red, with green tinsel and a reindeer stitched onto it. I bought it in a charity lucky dip – for £10 I could pick from a range of brown-paper parcels, each with a hand-decorated jumper inside. I think I lucked out with mine; it's over-the-top and silly without being too ugly. The Christmas party season starts for me when I get it out of my wardrobe, along with Christmas tree earrings, put it on and then pour myself a glass of Jingle Bell Fizz.

600ml / 1 pint cranberry juice drink, chilled
600ml / 1 pint apple juice, chilled
900ml / 1½ pints ginger beer, chilled
150ml / 5¼fl oz fresh lime juice
Lime wedges and fresh cranberries on picks, to garnish

1. Half-fill a large pitcher with ice. Pour in the cranberry juice, apple juice, and ginger beer. Squeeze in the lime juice. Gently stir to mix.

2. To serve, fill collins glasses with ice and pour in the mocktail. Garnish each glass with lime wedges and fresh cranberries threaded onto picks.

Zero-proof

Winter Sunrise

Serves 1

When you're a kid, Christmas Day starts in the dark. It's normally hours before the sun is due to rise and a lot earlier than your parents would like to be up. But once you've stirred from your sleep and felt the exciting weight of the presents Father Christmas has left, there's no avoiding getting up. As children, my sisters and I knew we should wait until at least 6am before running into our parents' room to let them know Santa had been. The time spent waiting felt like forever. I remember sitting by my bedroom window, looking out into the thick darkness and willing the sun to rise. But in England in December, the sun doesn't get up until 8am, so my wishes were all in vain. In the end, we'd open our presents lit up by bedside lamps and have eaten our breakfast and started playing with our new toys long before daylight stained the horizon. Once the sun was up, it meant it was time to get dressed because our relatives would soon be over and the celebrations would begin. The designated drivers used to make do with cups of tea and glasses of cola back then. I think they'd have enjoyed a glass of this bubbly, warmly spiced fruit mocktail more.

25ml / 1fl oz grenadine syrup
100ml / 3½fl oz fresh orange juice, chilled
60ml / 2fl oz ginger beer, chilled
Orange wheel and maraschino cherry on a pick, to garnish

1. Fill a highball glass with ice. Pour the grenadine into the glass, then top it up with the orange juice. Finish with the ginger beer. Don't stir to mix. The grenadine should sink into the bottom of the glass, staining the orange juice red and finally fading into the pale ginger beer.

2. Thread an orange wheel and maraschino cherry onto a pick and rest it on the rim of the glass to garnish. Serve with (optional) reusable straws – you can use them to mix the drink in the glass just before you drink it.

Zero-proof

Turkish Delight Lemonade

Serves 1

In Narnia, where it's always winter but never Christmas, eating Turkish delight is a risky business. The Turkish delight conjured by The White Witch is enchanted and 'anyone who had once tasted it would want more and more of it, and would even, if they were allowed, go on eating it until they killed themselves'. Unluckily, Edmund Pevensie doesn't find that out until it's too late and he is hopelessly under The White Witch's sway. Edmund's love of Turkish delight in CS Lewis' *The Lion, The Witch and The Wardrobe* leads him to betray his family and Aslan, almost ensuring the triumph of evil. But he realizes the error of his ways just in time and fights on the side of good – and Christmas – in the final battle. There's no clue in the book as to whether Edmund's craving for Turkish delight ever goes away. Given how much trouble it got him into, I wouldn't be surprised if just a whiff of sugar and roses gave him PTSD. Hopefully this floral sparkling lemonade won't turn you into a minion for evil. But I can't guarantee it. If it does, I trust the mouthwatering mix of citrus and perfumed petals was worth it.

30ml / 1fl oz Simple Syrup (see page 18)
1 tsp rose water
25ml / 1fl oz fresh lemon juice
15ml / ½fl oz fresh lime juice
80ml / 2½fl oz soda water, chilled
Turkish delight on a pick, to garnish

1. Pour the Simple Syrup, rose water, and lemon and lime juices into a cocktail shaker. Add a handful of ice, seal, then shake until the tin is frosty.

2. Fill a highball glass with ice. Pour in the rose-flavoured syrup. Top up with the chilled soda water and gently stir to mix.

3. Thread a couple of cubes of Turkish delight onto a cocktail pick and rest it on the rim of the glass. Serve with (optional) reusable straws.

Gingerman

Serves 1

My toddler niece and nephew's favourite treat is a gingerbread biscuit. They will accept a gingerbread heart, a gingerbread pig, or a gingerbread sheep, but their favourite is a 'ginger man'. Most cafés have some kind of ginger biscuit on offer throughout the year but at Christmas, when gingerbread is everywhere, they are in snack heaven. A toddlers' treat is a bit of a come-down for gingerbreadmen, which have royal origins. The first gingerbreadmen were served in the court of Elizabeth I. The English queen had a royal gingerbreadmaker as part of her retinue. For banquets, he'd bake little ginger-flavoured men in the image of her favourites and visiting dignitaries. Delicately moulded and decorated with gold leaf, they must have delighted and flattered their recipients. There's nothing like a ginger biscuit for making people happy. The spices typically found in gingerbread – cinnamon, cloves, ginger, and nutmeg – also make a great flavour for a drink. Adding a shot of Gingerbread Syrup (see page 19) to diet cola brings out the cola's crisp aromatics. It's a herbaceous mix, with plenty of bakehouse warmth.

35ml / 1¼fl oz Gingerbread Syrup (see page 19)
15ml / ½fl oz fresh lime juice
125ml / 4¼fl oz diet cola, chilled
Lime wedge, to garnish

1. Fill a highball glass with ice. Pour in the Gingerbread Syrup and lime juice. Stir them to mix.

2. Top up the glass with the chilled diet cola. Drop a lime wedge into the glass to garnish and serve.

Zero-proof

Home Alone

Serves 1

'Fuller, go easy on the Pepsi!' Kieran Culkin's character Fuller in *Home Alone* gets this warning because he's known to wet the bed after drinking too much Pepsi. His cousin Kevin (Macauley Culkin) is meant to share a bed with Fuller and is unhappy at the prospect, especially after watching him glug back the cola. It's one of the reasons Kevin ends up banished to the attic, where he stays forgotten while the family flies to Paris. As a bit of movie product placement, it has long legs – 25 years after the film was released, here I am using Pepsi to make a mocktail inspired by the Christmas classic. This zero-proof drink is tart and tangy. It has a deep, burgundy-red colour thanks to the cranberry juice, which also gives the mocktail a refreshing dryness. Even though it's made with cola, this mocktail isn't too sweet. Great for grownups who want something alcohol-free and not too syrupy.

75ml / 3fl oz cranberry juice drink
15ml / ½fl oz fresh lime juice
100ml / 3½fl oz Pepsi, chilled
Lime wedge, to garnish

1. Fill a highball glass with ice. Pour in the cranberry juice and lime juice. Stir them to mix.

2. Top up the glass with chilled Pepsi and gently stir to mix. Drop a lime wedge into the glass and serve.

Zero-proof

Pistachio & White Chocolate Milkshake

Serves 1

Over the past couple of years, pistachios have begun appearing everywhere. They're used to stuff croissants, as a filling in chocolate bars, and even to flavour drinks. One of the first products to nudge us towards pistachio in everything was a certain coffeeshop chain's pistachio latte. Launched in 2021 as a limited-edition holiday special, it was made with espresso, steamed milk, pistachio flavouring, and a brown butter topping. The latte was an immediate hit that now returns every winter. The idea of a creamy, pistachio-flavoured drink is very tempting, so I've used pistachio cream to make a sumptuous milkshake. Pistachio cream is the Gen Z alternative to hazelnut spread Nutella. Made with pistachios, vegetable oil, and sugar, it's a satin-soft, luscious spread that's a natural fit with white chocolate. Blended with milk and ice cream, it makes a sweetly nutty shake. Look out for pistachio cream from Italy, with at least 20 per cent pistachios for the best flavour.

- 50g / 1¾oz white chocolate
- 50g / 1¾oz pistachio cream
- 200g / 7oz vanilla ice cream
- 100ml / 3½fl oz full-fat milk
- Whipped cream, chopped pistachios, and grated white chocolate, to garnish

1. Melt the white chocolate in the microwave, checking it every 10–15 seconds and stirring until it has smoothly melted. If you don't have a microwave, break the chocolate into chunks and put them in a heatproof bowl. Set the bowl over a pan of steaming hot water (don't let the water touch the bowl) and warm, stirring, until the chocolate has melted.

2. Scrape the chocolate into a blender. Add the pistachio cream, vanilla ice cream, and milk. Whizz together until smooth and creamy.

3. Pour the milkshake into a collins glass. Top with whipped cream, chopped pistachios, and grated white chocolate to garnish. Serve immediately with reusable straws.

Cranberry & Pomegranate Nojito

Serves 1

In Greece, pomegranates are a symbol of Christmas. Associated with prosperity and rebirth, pomegranates – both real and decorative – pop up everywhere during the festive season. Pomegranate ornaments are hung on Christmas trees; they appear on the front of Christmas cards and are turned into tabletop decorations. Pomegranates also play an important part in New Year celebrations. Once the midnight chimes have struck, everyone in the house goes outside and then the first person to go back in smashes a pomegranate on the doorstep. Covering the front of a house with the tiny, jewel-like seeds is said to ensure it will be filled with wealth, health, and happiness in the following year. Pomegranates ripen and are harvested in October and November, so the holiday season is a good time of year to use them in your drinks. This zero-proof twist on a Mojito is made with fresh pomegranate seeds and mint muddled together, then topped up with pomegranate juice. A beautiful shade of ruby red and mouth-wateringly zesty, it's cool and refreshing.

10 fresh mint leaves
2 tbsp fresh pomegranate seeds
25ml / 1fl oz fresh lime juice
15ml / ½fl oz Cranberry Syrup (see page 19)
125ml / 4¼fl oz pomegranate juice drink
Mint sprig and pomegranate seeds, to garnish

1. Drop the mint leaves and pomegranate seeds into a collins glass and use a muddler to lightly crush them. The mint leaves should smell fragrant, and the seeds start to release their juice.

2. Pour in the lime juice and Cranberry Syrup. Fill the glass with crushed ice and use a bar spoon to churn together for 1 minute. Top up the ice and pour in the pomegranate juice. Churn to mix.

3. Tuck a mint sprig into the glass and scatter over a few pomegranate seeds. Serve with (optional) reusable straws.

Elves' Spiced Hot Chocolate

Serves 2

What makes a Christmas movie family-friendly changes over time. *The Santa Clause* opens with ad executive Scott Calvin accidentally killing Santa. His young son, Charlie, is unfazed by Santa's broken body and persuades his dad to don the red suit and spend the rest of Christmas Eve delivering presents. There's nothing more practical than a child when gifts are at risk. After returning the reindeer to the North Pole, Scott is given warm pyjamas and an elf named Judy makes him a reviving hot chocolate. She tells him: '(it's) my own recipe. It took me 12 hundred years to get it right'. Judy's secrets include extra chocolate and shaking rather than stirring. I think shaking hot liquids is risky for mere mortals, so I've whisked to add air and lightness. I've also added extra chocolate as well as cocoa powder to ensure the drink is plush and luxurious. Cozily reassuring, with a hint of cinnamon, this is a hot chocolate to restore anyone's spirits, whether they're tired from Christmas shopping or burying mythical creatures in the garden.

75g / 3oz dark chocolate, 80% cocoa solids
75g / 3oz milk chocolate
1 tbsp cocoa powder
2 tbsp soft brown sugar
500ml / 17½fl oz full-fat milk
100ml / 3½fl oz double cream
1 tsp vanilla extract
1 tsp ground cinnamon
Whipped cream and grated chocolate, to serve

1. Roughly chop the dark and milk chocolates and scoop them into a small pan. Add the cocoa powder and soft brown sugar.

2. Pour in the milk and double cream, then add the vanilla and cinnamon. Set the pan over a medium heat and gently warm, whisking, until the chocolate has melted and smoothly combined.

3. Ladle the hot chocolate into two heatproof glasses or mugs. Top with whipped cream and grate over a little chocolate to serve.

Midwinter Mull

Serves 6

Mulled drinks have been a part of midwinter celebrations for centuries. The word 'mull' itself started being used in the early 1600s. It meant to heat, sweeten, and flavour with spices. And in Northern Europe, where the climate was heavy on snow and ice while the fires only warmed the hearth for so long, hot drinks would have felt like a celebration every time you took a sip. Non-alcoholic alternatives to Mulled Wine tend to focus on just one juice, like cranberry or apple. This warming, zero-proof punch is a mix of orange juice for sweetness and pomegranate for tang. It takes the flavour a little bit closer to Mulled Wine by making sure there's a touch of tartness to the finished drink. It's flavoured with a mix of spices and a fragrant Mulled Syrup (see page 18). Along with the citrus fruit, they round out the flavours and give it a festive warmth. Ladle it into mugs and serve by a fire. Indoors, it feels snug and comforting. It's also great for keeping you warm if you're outside by a bonfire. Wrap your hands around the mug and enjoy the soothing glow.

- 750ml / 1⅓ pints pomegranate juice
- 750ml / 1⅓ pints fresh orange juice
- 75ml / 3fl oz Mulled Syrup (see page 18)
- 1 orange
- 1 lemon
- 1 lime
- 24 whole cloves
- 2 cinnamon sticks

1. Pour the pomegranate juice, orange juice, and Mulled Syrup into a large pan.

2. Slice the orange, lemon, and lime. Stud a couple of the fruit slices with the cloves, then add them all to the pan. Drop in the cinnamon sticks.

3. Set the pan over a medium heat, pop on a lid and bring to the boil, then turn the heat down and simmer for 10 minutes to infuse the drink. Taste the warm punch and add a little more Mulled Syrup if you think it needs it.

4. Ladle the Mull into heatproof glasses or mugs and serve immediately.

Zero-proof

Index

A
aquafaba or egg whites 14

B
Baby Eggnog 123
Baddest Santa 72
bar spoon types 7
Beer Syrup 20, 79
bitters 14
blenders 9
Blushing Elf 39
Buon Natale 32

C
Candy Cane Martini 52
Christmapolitan 103
Christmas Kiss 92
Christmas in New York 64
Christmas on the Beach 107
Christmas Past 36
Christmas Star 115
Cinnamon Roll Martini 79
citrus twists 12–13
citrus wheels, slices, and wedges 13
Clementine Margarita 56
cocktail shaker types 6–7
Cranberry Christmas Mule 43
Cranberry & Pomegranate Nojito 136
Cranberry Syrup 19, 36, 52, 107, 112, 115, 136

DE
Eggnog 108
egg whites or aquafaba 16
Elves' Spiced Hot Chocolate 139
express a twist, how to 13

F
Flip 36
Frozen Cranberry Daiquiris 112

G
garnishes 12–13
garnishing tools 9
  canele cutter 9
  channel knife 9
Gingerbread Old Fashioned 24
Gingerbread Syrup 19, 24, 87, 96, 131
Gingerman 131
glassware 10–12
Guinness Syrup 21, 27, 59

H
Hanukkah 48
Home Alone 132
Home for the Holidays 116
Honey Buttered Rum 99
Hot Toddy 96

I
ice cube trays 9

J
jiggers 8
Jingle Bell Fizz 124
juicers 9

K
Kwanzaa 68

LM
Marzipan Sour 31
measuring glasses 8
Mele Kalikimaka 44

Midwinter Mull 140
mixing glasses 7
mocktails 122–141
Mrs Claus's Secret 75
muddlers 8
Mulled Spritz 84
Mulled Syrup 18, 64, 84, 140
Mulled Wine 120

N
Naughty & Nice Shots 119
New Year's Eve 87
North Pole Martini 111
Nutcracker 80

O
Olive Oil Martini 48
Out of Office 91

P
Pear & Ginger Bellini 87
pear purée 86
Pineapple Syrup 20, 68, 71
Pistachio & White Chocolate Milkshake 135
pitcher drinks 102–121
Polar Espresso Martini 63

QR
Recipes, The 22–141
Red & Green Heart 71
rim a glass, how to 14
Rudolph's Rocket Fuel 55
Rudolph's Rum Swizzle 47
Rye Hard 27

S
Saint Nick 83
salt a glass, how to 4
Sangría Navideña 104
Santa's Sidecar 67
Santa's Smash 35

Simple Syrup 16, 18, 23, 35, 40, 47, 56, 72, 76, 103, 108, 123, 128
Small Town Hottie 96
smoke a cocktail, how to 14
Snow Day 23
Snowflake 88
Snow Globe 40
Snow in the City 60
Spritz 11, 84
Staying up for the Solstice 59
sterilizing jars and bottles 17
St Louis-style Whiskey Punch 68
strainers 8
Stuck up the Chimney 28
Sugar Cookie Cocktail 51
sugar rim a glass, how to 14
syrups 17–21
  Beer Syrup 20, 79
  Cranberry Syrup 19, 36, 52, 107, 112, 115, 136
  Gingerbread Syrup 119, 24, 87, 96, 131
  Guinness Syrup 21, 27, 59
  Mulled Syrup 18, 64, 84, 140
  Pineapple Syrup 20, 68, 71
  Simple Syrup 16, 18, 23, 35, 40, 47, 56, 72, 76, 103, 108, 123, 128

T
Tipsy Snowman 95
tools and equipment 6–9
Turkish Delight Lemonade 128

UV
Under the Mistletoe 76

W
White Christmas 100
Winter Sunrise 127

XYZ
zero-proof 122–141

Acknowledgements

To my editor Caitlin Doyle, who recognized a fellow Christmas nerd and gave me the chance to indulge in all my favourite Christmas themes. Hannah Wood, whose illustrations have beautifully captured the spirit of Christmas. Helena Caldon, for her sharp copyediting skills and for sharing the fact that there's an app that can count the days down to Christmas. To all the team at HarperCollins who have worked so hard on this book. And to my friends and family, who've always made Christmas a magical time of year. Especially Mum, Dad, Alex, Cara, Liam, Niamh and the hosts of our annual Friends' 'Fakemas': Fran, Jordi, Jennie, and Nicola.